FEARLESS FOOD

For Cian, Marco & Clara,
wherever you may roam.

FEARLESS FOOD

LYNDA BOOTH

DCS
PUBLISHING

INTRODUCTION

Food has many functions. It is a source of pleasure, a means of soothing, an outlet for emotion, an opportunity for communication. In recent years, there has been increasing focus on just one function: food as a set of nutrients to keep us in good health. We are bombarded with messages of what we should eat and, more usually, what we should not; by claims and counterclaims; by information and misinformation. The result is that many of us now shop and eat in a state of alert. This is fostered by a food media who have been hijacked by allergists, diet fanatics and celebrities promoting a particular lifestyle. This book aims to be an antidote to that trend. The food here is "accidentally healthy", one of the more hopeful food phrases of recent times. The aim is that we might cook more and analyse less. Food changes if we can separate it from the realm of threat. It becomes joyful, something we want to share.

This is an invitation to celebrate the sight of opening a fish parcel, the taste of spices released into a curry, the smells of a braise wafting through the kitchen or the feel of uncurling a cinnamon roll. It's time to get back to cooking without fear. It's time for fearless food.

CONTENTS

BRUNCH

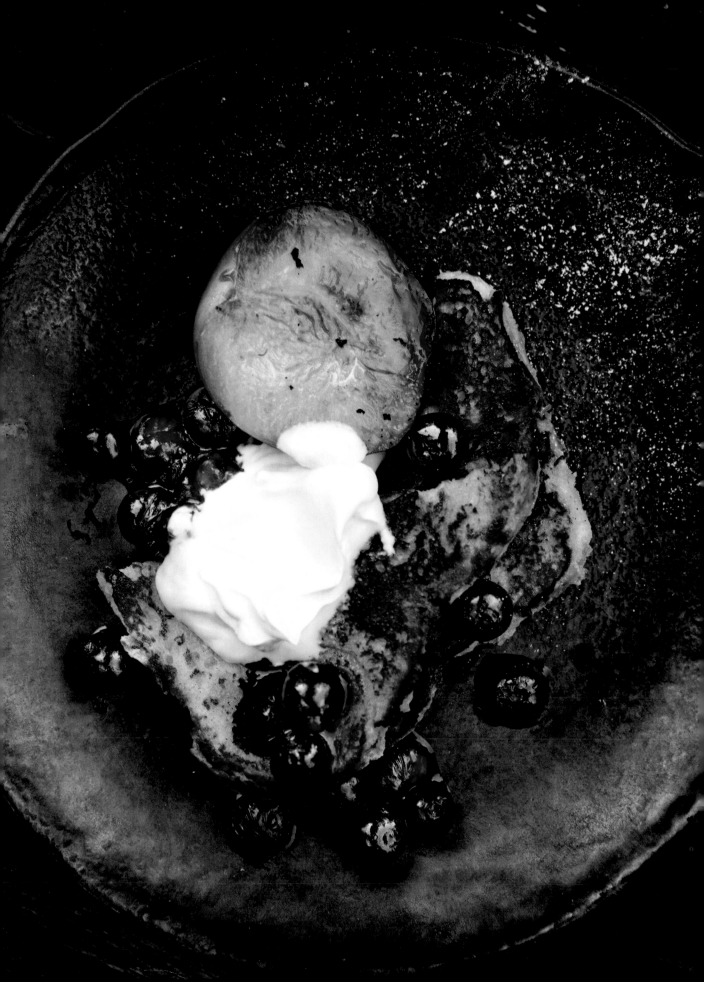

BRUNCH

Brunch can be what you like. My preference, when I have the time, is for a lingering meal, unravelling slowly with new dishes arriving periodically. Most of the preparation can be done the previous day or when you would have breakfasted that morning. This affords an ease to the cooking when everyone has arrived: some stirring, cracking a few eggs, shifting dishes in and out of the oven. For me, a brunch needs to have some form and some balance. In order to keep myself in line, I think of three things. It needs fruit, perhaps poached, with something acidic like natural yoghurt. It needs something savoury, often with an egg nestling in there somewhere, and it needs something sweet, a waft of fresh baking to the table. For a long brunch, I don't want to fill up completely on the savouries because I have to make it through to the sweet conclusion - that's the best bit.

Previous page: Brioche french toast, nectarines & blueberries - page 54

BAKED PLUMS	15
VANILLA YOGHURT & GRANOLA	
CHORIZO & CANNELLINI BEAN STEW	19
GARLIC & CHILLI BREAD	
AVOCADO SMASH ON BRUSCHETTA	22
CHILLI & MINT OIL, POACHED EGG & FETA	
KEDGEREE	25
SHAKSHUKA	28
CRISPY EGG, SALAD WITH LARDONS & CAPERS	30
PAN FRIED BLACK PUDDING	
KOREAN PANCAKE	34
SOY & CHILLI DIP	
PARISIAN PITTA & ACCOMPANIMENTS	37
FALAFEL, TAHINA, PICKLED CUCUMBER	40
SPICY RATATOUILLE, TAHINA	45
BEEF BOURGUIGNON, PICKLED SHALLOTS	47
MULTISEED BROWN YEAST BREAD	51
RICOTTA PANCAKES	52
MIXED BERRIES	
BUTTERMILK PANCAKES	
BRIOCHE FRENCH TOAST	54
NECTARINES & BLUEBERRIES	
RASPBERRY BRIOCHE BUNS	55
CINNAMON BUNS	58

BAKED PLUMS
VANILLA YOGHURT & GRANOLA

Finding ripe plums isn't always easy but baking them in the oven releases their natural juices and provides a fruity syrup which can be spooned over fresh yoghurt. Sprinkle over some granola, preferably homemade, and you have a great start to a brunch. There are good granolas on the market but you can't beat choosing your own balance of ingredients. With the quantities below, there will be plenty left for another day.

Serves 6

GRANOLA
150g jumbo oats
60g pumpkin seeds
60g sunflower seeds
40g flaked unsweetened coconut
100g pecans
50g unsalted butter (or coconut oil)
½ tsp cinnamon
90ml maple syrup (or agave syrup)
pinch salt

FOR THE PLUMS & YOGHURT
9 plums, cut in half and the stone
   removed
400ml Greek yoghurt
2 vanilla pods
75g castor sugar
6 tbsp water
a little honey, to taste

Preheat oven to 170°C, 150°C Fan, 325°F, Gas 3.

Granola
Line a baking tray with a silicone mat or parchment paper. Place the first four ingredients in a bowl, chop the pecans roughly into about 3 pieces and add to the mix. Melt the butter in a medium saucepan, add the cinnamon, maple syrup and a pinch of salt. Add the dry ingredients to the saucepan and mix well. Spread the granola onto the lined baking tray. Pop in the oven to roast lightly for about 20 minutes, turning once with a spatula during the cooking process. Remove, allow to cool and store in an airtight jar.

Increase the temperature of the oven for the plums to 200°C, 180°C fan, 400°F, Gas 6.

To prepare the plums & yoghurt
Place the plums in a single layer in an ovenproof dish. Pour the yoghurt into a serving bowl. Split the vanilla pods in half lengthways. Using a small utility knife, flatten the pods with a knife and scrape out the little black seeds. Scatter the seeds from one pod over the plums and add the seeds from the second pod to the yoghurt. Add the shells of the two pods to the plums, sprinkle over 75g sugar and pour in the water. Cover the plums with tinfoil and bake in a preheated oven for about 20-30 minutes, depending on their ripeness.

Mix the honey into the yoghurt and vanilla. Keep refrigerated until ready to use.

Serve the baked plums warm or cold (they can be reheated in the oven if you wish) along with the syrup. Spoon over the vanilla yoghurt and scatter some granola on top.

CHORIZO & CANNELLINI BEAN STEW
GARLIC & CHILLI BREAD

This is one of the fastest tracks to deliciousness. The three key ingredients are all Spanish: a chorizo sausage, some piquillo peppers and some paprika. If you have these to hand, you are ready to go. It's amazing how the spiciness of the chorizo and the paprika breathe life into the cannellini beans. Starting off with ciabatta or a crusty loaf from a market, the chilli in the butter provides a jolt and then a contrasting heat with the milder spicing of the beans.

Serves 4

GARLIC & CHILLI BREAD

3 cloves garlic, crushed

25g parsley, chopped

1 spring onion, finely chopped

100g butter, at room temperature

2 tbsp olive oil

3 tsp chilli powder

1 ciabatta loaf or baguette,
  about 280g

50g Parmesan, grated

CANNELLINI BEAN STEW

1 tbsp olive oil

1 onion, finely chopped
  (or 2 shallots)

1 clove of garlic, sliced

1 sprig of thyme

1 dried red chilli, left whole

100g chorizo, chopped into fine dice

8 piquillo peppers or 3 roasted
  red peppers, peeled (see overleaf)

1 tsp smoked paprika

a pinch of chilli flakes

2 x 400g tin cannellini beans

200ml chicken, vegetable stock
  or Marigold bouillon

1 tbsp crème fraîche

chopped parsley or coriander,
  to garnish

Preheat the oven to 200°C, 180°C Fan, 400°F, Gas 6.

Garlic & chilli bread

Mix the garlic, parsley and spring onion together. Add the butter, olive oil and chilli powder and mash together with a fork or a wooden spoon. Mix until all the ingredients are blended together. Split the baguette or ciabatta loaf in half. Spread a thick layer of the garlic and chilli butter on the cut side of the bread and top with Parmesan cheese. Wrap in tinfoil and bake in the oven for 15 minutes. Unwrap the foil and leave in the oven for about 5 minutes until the Parmesan browns a little. Serve immediately. If not using straight away, keep wrapped in the tinfoil.

Cannellini bean stew

Heat a saucepan over medium heat. Drizzle in the oil and when hot, add the chopped onion. Season with salt, turn down the heat to low, cover and cook for about 5 minutes or until the onions are translucent and completely tender. Stir a few times during the cooking. Add the garlic, thyme and dried chilli and continue to cook for another 30 seconds before adding the diced chorizo. Cook over a low heat until the oil releases from the chorizo and the onions become a lovely rusty color. Chop the piquillo peppers or roasted peppers into strips and add to the pot along with smoked paprika and a pinch of chilli flakes (if you wish). Continue to cook for a few minutes to allow the flavours to infuse. Strain and rinse the cannellini beans, discarding the liquid. Add the beans to the saucepan, along with the stock. Simmer gently for about 5 minutes. Just before serving, spoon in the crème fraîche. Taste to check the seasoning. Remove the sprig of thyme and the dried chilli.

Serve in a bowl along with the chilli bread. Garnish with chopped parsley or coriander. Salsa verde, pesto or pickled shallots add another flourish at the end if you have any in your fridge.

Roasting peppers in the oven

Preheat the oven to 240°C, 220°C Fan, 475°F, Gas 9.

Place the peppers on a baking tray. Roast in the oven for about 30 minutes until they become partially blackened and the skin becomes blistered. Remove from the oven. Using the tip of a small knife, peel away the skin and discard. It's easier to peel the peppers as soon as they emerge from the oven as the skin comes away in much bigger pieces. When cool, remove the core, cut them in half and scrape away the seeds. Cut into strips and use as directed.

PIQUILLO PEPPERS

Piquillo peppers are small red chillis prized for their sweetness rather than heat. They are grown extensively in Northern Spain where they are roasted over embers and then peeled, deseeded, packed in tins or jars and covered with olive oil. They impart a fruity and smoky flavour. They are one of my favourite store cupboard ingredients.

AVOCADO SMASH ON BRUSCHETTA
CHILLI & MINT OIL
POACHED EGG & FETA

A bruschetta is a great base for so many brunch ideas. If I can find really ripe avocados (or bring them home to ripen), then they can be mashed up into a creamy consistency and drizzled with an oil that has both the heat of some chilli and the freshness of some mint. Top this with a poached egg and some sharp, salty feta cheese.

Serves 4

CHILLI & MINT OIL
1 green chilli
a sliver of crushed garlic
20 mint leaves
4 tbsp olive oil

AVOCADO SMASH
4 ripe avocados
2 spring onions, finely chopped
pinch of chilli flakes
1 tbsp lime juice
salt

4 slices ciabatta or sourdough bread
a clove of garlic
olive oil, for the bruschetta
40g-60g feta cheese

4 large eggs

Chilli & mint oil
Chop the green chilli roughly, leaving the seeds in if preferred. Whizz the chilli, garlic and mint leaves to a paste in a small spice grinder (or chop the chilli and mint as finely as you can). Add the olive oil, season with salt and transfer to a small container.

Avocado smash
Cut the avocados in half and remove the stone. With a large spoon, scoop out the flesh into a mixing bowl. Using a fork, mash the avocado roughly, but still leaving some fairly big chunks. Add the spring onions, chilli flakes, lime juice and 2 tablespoons of chilli and mint oil. Mix and season with salt. If not using immediately, press clingfilm directly on the surface to prevent oxidisation and refrigerate.

Heat a griddle pan and char the bread lightly on both sides. Alternatively, toast under the grill. Rub a cut clove garlic lightly, once or twice, over the bread and drizzle with a little extra virgin olive oil. Scoop the avocado smash on top, spoon over some chilli and mint oil, and crumble over some feta.

Poaching eggs
Meanwhile, bring a large pot of water to the boil. Using a hand whisk, swirl the water and turn down to a gentle simmer. Break the eggs one by one into a ramekin or small bowl and gently tip them into the water. Up to 4 eggs can be cooked at the same time. As soon as they have been added to the pot, turn off the heat and cover with a lid. For runny yolks, the eggs will need 3-4 minutes, depending on their size. No peeking until 3 minutes have passed. Remove with a slotted spoon and drain on kitchen paper or a tea cloth. Place the egg on top of the avocado and serve immediately.

HASSLE-FREE EGG POACHING

It works a treat if you are having friends around to poach eggs in advance and then to reheat them in barely simmering water. Cook the eggs as above, making sure the yolks are nice and runny and scoop them them directly into a bowl of ice cold water. They may be stored in water in the fridge for a couple of days. Reheat in barely simmering water for about 30 seconds. A useful tip is to use eggs that are as fresh as possible so the whites do not become straggly.

KEDGEREE

Every month our full-time students run a pop-up restaurant in the cookery school. For many it's their first experience of feeling the adrenaline of a team working flat out to produce something memorable and then celebrating together afterwards. The following day is a late start and we get slowly into our stride with brunch. We have tried many options but nothing has proved as soothing for heads and stomachs as an old-fashioned kedgeree. You could try a vegetarian version with rice, lentils and onions which is comforting in its own way, but somehow the smoked fish hits the spot like nothing else. It is not essential to be hungover to enjoy this dish.

Serves 4-6

4-6 medium eggs,
   at room temperature

600g-800g smoked haddock fillet,
   skin on

400ml chicken stock, Marigold
   bouillon or water

300g basmati rice

25g butter

2 tsp cumin seeds

6 green cardamom pods,
   very lightly crushed

1 cinnamon stick

3 cloves

1 onion, peeled and finely chopped

1 tbsp medium curry powder,
   such as Sharwoods

½ tsp ground turmeric

½ tsp salt

200g peas

a small handful of freshly
   chopped coriander or parsley

squeeze of lemon juice

lemon wedges, to serve

shallow fried onions, optional
   (see overleaf)

For the eggs

Bring a large pot of water to the boil. Gently lower the eggs into the water and cook for 5½ minutes. Remove from the water and place in cold water to stop them cooking. Allow to cool. Peel and set aside until ready to serve.

For the kedgeree

Put the smoked haddock in a saucepan and add the stock. Simmer over a low heat for 5 minutes and then leave to stand, covered, for 10 minutes. Strain, reserving the fish and cooking broth. Rinse the rice in a bowl of cold water and drain.

Heat a saucepan and add the butter. When the butter is foaming, add the cumin seeds, cardamom pods, cinnamon stick and cloves. Cook for about 10 seconds and then add the onion. Season, turn down the heat to low and cover with a lid. Sweat the onions for about 10 minutes or until softened. Stir in the curry powder and turmeric followed by the basmati rice. Pour the fish poaching liquid into a measuring jug and add enough water to make up to 700ml. Pour the contents of the jug over the rice, add ½ teaspoon of salt, bring to the boil and cover tightly with a lid. Reduce the heat to a minimum and cook gently for 15 minutes. Remove the lid and taste a few grains of rice. If the rice is tender, turn off the heat.

Meanwhile, remove the skin and bones from the smoked haddock. Flake the fish into small chunks. Blanch the peas in boiling water for a couple of minutes. Fold the fish and peas into the rice, add some chopped coriander or parsley and a good squeeze of lemon juice. Leave to sit for 5-10 minutes with the lid on. Fluff up the grains of rice with a fork and check the seasoning. To warm the eggs, lower them gently into a pot of boiling water for about 20 seconds.

Place the kedgeree in a warmed serving bowl. Slice the eggs in half and sit them on top. Garnish with some extra coriander or parsley and some shallow fried onions, if using.

SHALLOW FRIED ONIONS

Shallow fried onions are an optional garnish which provide texture.

1 onion, sliced into half moons
  about 0.5cm thick
30g plain flour
vegetable or sunflower oil for
  deep-frying

Line a tray with kitchen paper. Toss the sliced onion in plain flour. Fill a wok or deep saucepan half full with oil. Heat the oil until moderately hot (approximately 180°C, 350°F), then add the onions - be careful as the oil will bubble up. When the oil has recovered its heat, turn it down slightly. Deep fry, stirring constantly with tongs or a slotted spoon, until the onions turn golden. Place on the lined tray and season with salt. They will hold for a couple of days in an airtight container.

SHAKSHUKA

If it's good enough for half of the Middle East, you can be fairly sure that this will be pretty special. The pepper mixture can be made in advance (even a day or two before) so that all you have to do is reheat it and push back little pockets into which the eggs can be cracked. It is an impressive pan to bring to the table with the vivid colours of the peppers, the subtle scents of the cumin, paprika and saffron, and the anticipation of the quivering eggs. You can be pretty flexible as to what goes in – some cannellini beans from one of your previous triumphs, some chorizo or some feta cheese crumbled over the top – since shakshuka was originally a way of eating what was left over from the previous evening. It is best devoured with a fork in one hand and bread in the other.

Serves 4-5

pinch saffron, about 16 threads
2 tbsp olive oil
1 tsp cumin seeds
2 onions, sliced
2 bay leaves
¼ tsp chilli flakes
2 red peppers, cut into thin strips
1 green pepper, cut into thin strips
1 yellow pepper, cut into thin strips
1 x 400g tin chopped tomatoes
1 rounded tsp brown sugar
½ tsp smoked paprika

4-5 large eggs
freshly chopped coriander or parsley
   to garnish (optional)

To make the pepper base

Place the saffron in a small bowl and cover with 100ml boiling water. Leave to infuse. Heat the oil in a deep frying pan. When hot, add in the cumin seeds and after about 5-10 seconds when they go a shade darker, slide the onions into the pan. Season with salt, add the bay leaves, stir to mix and cover the pan. Cook at a medium heat for about 10 minutes until the onions have softened. Add in the chilli flakes and peppers, season and cook at a medium heat for 10 minutes with the lid on.

Mix the tinned tomatoes into the peppers along with the sugar, smoked paprika, saffron and the saffron water. Cook at a brisk heat for about 20 minutes, adding a little water if necessary until the tomatoes reduce to a thickish sauce. Taste and adjust the seasoning. The pepper mixture may be made up to this point in advance. It will keep in the fridge for several days.

To cook the eggs

Create 4 or 5 wells around the pan. Break the eggs, one by one, into a well. Cover the pan with a lid and cook for about 6 minutes or until the white is just set and the yolk still runny. Keep checking during the process as the timing of the eggs will vary. Scatter with chopped coriander or parsley and serve immediately. The eggs will carry on cooking if left in the pan, so don't sit there looking at them!

NOTE If cooking for larger numbers, it is best to divide the shakshuka into separate pans. The eggs cook more evenly if they are not spread out over too wide an area.

CRISPY EGG
SALAD WITH LARDONS & CAPERS
PAN FRIED BLACK PUDDING

Stephen Gibson, owner and head chef of *Pichet* restaurant in the centre of Dublin, is laid back, unflappable and full of stories. I well remember the first time I had one of his crispy eggs, so perfectly cooked that when I cut through the crunchy exterior, the soft oozing yolk was revealed. Perfection. I love it with black pudding but a few lardons of bacon on their own would also be wonderful with the frisée lettuce. Stephen generally has a squeezy bottle full of homemade mayonnaise which he squirts around the plate. If you fancy a shortcut, whisk a little extra virgin olive oil into regular mayonnaise with a hint of crushed garlic and some wholegrain mustard and give vent to your artistic side.

Serves 4

4 large free range eggs
   (plus a couple extra for breakage)
1 slice Parma ham
1 egg, mixed with a dash of milk
50g seasoned flour
100g Panko (see note overleaf)
   or regular breadcrumbs

FOR THE SALAD
100g smoked or unsmoked
   bacon lardons, or pancetta
30ml sherry vinegar
30g baby capers
4 tbsp extra virgin olive oil

60ml mayonnaise, bought or
   homemade (see overleaf)
2 tsp wholegrain mustard

220g black pudding
sunflower oil, for frying
handful of frisée lettuce,
   white part only or mixed leaves

To prepare the eggs
Bring a pot of water to a gentle simmer and lower the eggs gently into the water. (Perhaps cook a few extra eggs in case they break when peeling). Boil for 5 minutes, remove from the water and add to a bowl of cold or iced water. Crack each egg on the counter, on the wider end only, and return to the cold water. This helps release the shell when you are peeling it. Leave to sit in the water till cold. Peel very carefully and place on a plate, lined with clingfilm, in a single layer. Cut 4 strips of Parma ham about 3cm x 14cm. Dry the eggs with kitchen paper, handling them gently. Wrap a strip of Parma around the centre of each egg. Place three bowls on the counter, one with the beaten egg, the second with flour and the third with breadcrumbs. Dip each egg, firstly into the beaten egg, then the flour, followed by the breadcrumbs. Lay the eggs on a tray or plate lined with clingfilm. The eggs may be dipped in advance and left in the fridge until ready to serve. It is best to bring them back to room temperature about an hour in advance before deep frying.

For the salad
Heat a small non-stick pan, add a dash of sunflower oil and when hot, add the bacon lardons. Cook at a brisk heat, tossing continuously until the fat renders out and the bacon becomes crisp. If there is excess fat in the pan, wipe out with kitchen paper. Deglaze the pan with sherry vinegar, boil to reduce for a few seconds, then toss in the capers. Remove from the heat and drizzle in the olive oil. Allow to cool. The dressing may be prepared ahead of time.

Mix the mayonnaise and wholegrain mustard together and set aside.

Slice the black pudding about 1cm or 1.5cm thick. Heat a little olive oil in the pan and when hot, add the slices of black pudding. Cook for a few minutes until lightly coloured on the underside, turn over and repeat on the other side. Set aside while you deep fry the eggs.

Deep frying the eggs

Heat a generous amount of sunflower oil in a wok, saucepan or deep fat fryer. Line a tray with kitchen paper and leave it beside the hob. Bring the oil up to a temperature of 170°C, 325°F. If you do not have a thermometer, check the temperature of the oil by dropping a piece of bread into it. It should go golden in 15-20 seconds. If the oil is too hot, allow to cool a little before using. Deep fry the eggs for 30-45 seconds until they are golden and crispy on the outside. Drain on kitchen paper. Place a dessertspoon of mayonnaise on the plate and spread with the back of the spoon. Arrange the black pudding on the plate and scatter over a few pieces of frisée or mixed lettuce. Spoon over some of the caper sherry vinaigrette. Cut the egg in half and sit alongside or on top of the black pudding.

NOTE Panko breadcrumbs are fine crispy breadcrumbs available in Asian markets. They have a long shelf life.

MAYONNAISE

2 egg yolks
1 tbsp white wine vinegar
¼ tsp Dijon mustard
230ml sunflower oil
70ml olive oil
squeeze of lemon juice
¼ tsp salt

Place the egg yolks in a bowl with the vinegar and mustard. Using a hand or an electric whisk (electric is preferable), whisk in the oil in a cautious trickle at first, then gradually building up to a steady stream. The mayonnaise will become thicker as the oil is poured in. Finish by adding the olive oil and a squeeze of lemon juice. Season with salt to taste.

If the mixture curdles (the mayonnaise becomes runny and does not thicken despite the addition of oil), place 1 egg yolk in a clean bowl and pour in the curdled mayonnaise drop by drop, whisking as you go.

To make in a food processor or liquidiser

Use 1 whole egg instead of the egg yolks. Put the whole egg, vinegar, mustard and salt into a liquidiser or food processor. Turn on the machine and then slowly add the oil through the hole in the lid until you have a thick emulsion.

WHY COOK?

I think this is a great question. If we are going to eat at least a couple of times a day then surely our attitude to cooking is worth serious consideration.

If we don't cook, then there are of course consequences. Since we have to eat, the risk is of an inevitable drift towards processed foods. Parts of the food industry relish this. While it may be convenient that they would take apart natural foods and then reinvent them in a less perishable (and more lucrative) way, this is the public health disaster that is growing in our society. We are also likely to increase our takeaway meal consumption. I'm more than happy to flag up the health cost of fast food - the reliable Safefood site breaks down what you are actually consuming in a takeaway in a fairly sobering fashion.

Half-hearted cooking may lead to better food than ready meals but the personal cost can be high. It is often inefficient and energy-sapping. It may involve not knowing what you want to eat, shopping at the last minute, cobbling something together and then feeling unappreciated. If you feel your shortcomings as a cook are also under constant exposure, it can easily become dispiriting.

However, when we really engage with cooking then many good things tend to follow. Shopping becomes more interesting as you look for things to inspire. There is a satisfaction as you become better able to hold a whole recipe in mind so that ingredients are prepared in order and are at hand. Opportunities may be taken to cook more than you need so that the fridge and freezer are being used for quick turnarounds. There may be occasional longer sessions of cooking at a time that suits so that you can get ahead of yourself for a few days. Even on a busy day, you have the reward of seeing others enjoy what you have prepared for them.

While the preparation and cooking of food can be daunting at first, confidence increases the pleasure over time. Cooking becomes more intuitive and creative. When you open the fridge, you see possibilities. When you have something to start with, it becomes easier to rustle up meals with what is there. You know what can be left out, what can be substituted and what might very well work. Cooking can become a blast.

Passionate cooking takes no more time than listless cooking and it is time of a quite different quality. If you embrace cooking, you are less likely to ruminate about food and just enjoy eating it. Food writer Diana Henry refers to food becoming "accidentally healthy" – it just happens to do you good rather than that being the sole intention. Cooking means that you take control of what you eat and makes it more likely that you sit down with others. This is not just good for your health, it's good for your soul.

KOREAN PANCAKE
SOY & CHILLI DIP

Tara Livingston joined us as a tutor direct from a two year stint as a chef in Paris. She and her fellow chefs would often meet up at midday on a Sunday to cook for each other and compare notes from the week. There was one Korean in the group and they were intrigued as to what his contribution would be to their brunch. He stunned them all with this pancake. Slightly charred at a brisk heat, it becomes crisp on the outside while the vegetables retain a slight bite. The soy dip that is spooned over the top traditionally has a chilli powder added to it called "gochugaru" which apart from having a name worth buying, really does add a unique distinctive smoky taste. Presuming that this is not easily to hand, substitute a regular chilli powder or my own favoured brand, Deggi Mirch (see page 248), which is widely available in Asian markets. The Korean dip is wonderful spooned over white fish (see page 189) or chicken so it is no harm to make a double batch so that you have a little stash in the fridge.

Serves 6
Makes 6 x 18cm pancakes

KOREAN DIP
100g Kikkoman soy sauce
20g sugar
1 tbsp "gochugaru" or 1 tsp
   chilli powder
40g shallot, diced very finely
2 spring onions, sliced finely
2 tsp sesame seeds
40g water

KOREAN PANCAKE MIX
120g plain flour
120g rice flour
2 eggs
240ml cold water
pinch salt

FILLING
6 spring onions
2 large carrots (about 220g)
2 medium courgettes (360g)
100g onion
2 green chillies

sunflower oil, for frying

Korean dip
Mix all the ingredients together. Store in a jam jar in the fridge. This dip will hold for up to a month.

To make the Korean pancakes
Place the flour and rice flour in a bowl. Make a well in the centre and whisk in the eggs and water to make a thickish batter. The amount of liquid may vary slightly with different flours. Season with salt.

Chop the spring onions into 4cm pieces. Slice the carrot into julienne (thin matchstick strips). Halve the courgette lengthwise and then slice thinly about 2-3mm thick. Slice the onion in half and then lengthways into very thin strips. Slice the chilli peppers thinly crossways.

For each pancake, place a handful of vegetables, about 150g, into a bowl and pour over about 100g batter (there should be a small amount of onion compared to everything else). The idea is to just coat the vegetables in the batter so that they stick together. They should not be going for a swim. Mix well using a spatula.

Heat a non-stick frying pan and pour a thin layer of sunflower oil over the base of the pan (about 3 tablespoons). Pour the vegetable and batter mix into the pan and spread out to make a thick pancake. Cook at a brisk heat until the edges are beginning to colour and the vegetables char a little on the underside. Flip the pancake and cook for another few minutes. Serve immediately, cut into wedges. Spoon some Korean dip over each slice.

PARISIAN PITTA
FALAFEL & ACCOMPANIMENTS

It sounds very grand to have a favourite walk in Paris. I have an excuse - I have a son who lives there. Though I may get distracted away from my usual path, by the time I get to the Jewish quarter in Le Marais, I always end up on the street with the best falafel in the world. How do I know? Well it has to be a bit special when you see the haughty Parisians joining the throng of tourists in a queue stretching half way down the street.

The exuberant owners have gone to great lengths to work out the extraordinary combination of textures and tastes that get stuffed into the pitta bread that make them so memorable. Aside from the spicy falafel, there is the tahini sauce, the crunchy red cabbage, the soft texture of the aubergines, the pickled cucumber, the pickled shallots and the yoghurt dressing. I have gone to great lengths to get the full recipe in stages, one innocent question at a time. It is your job to work out when this spread might fit the bill. I have found that it works really well if a big scrum of people are due to arrive nearer lunch than breakfast. There is some preparation but many of the elements can be kept for long periods in the fridge and so, once made, can be drawn on as required.

One final point - pitta bread is readily available to buy but these are usually too thin to hold much of a filling. I urge you to try making them yourself. They are light, soft and fluffy, hold a mountain of fillings without falling apart and become a significant element in the whole experience. A pizza stone gives great results but the pitta may also be cooked on a hot baking tray. They even freeze well which is why I have included three options with widely contrasting fillings. Hang on tight for three long (but really rewarding) recipes!

PITTA BREAD
300-400ml warm water
10g fresh yeast or 1½ tsp dried yeast
500g strong white flour
1½ tsp salt
1 tsp sugar
2 tbsp olive oil

Place 200ml warm water in a jug and sprinkle on the yeast. Stir and leave for about 5 minutes to activate.

Making the dough in a mixer
If you have a stand mixer, place the flour, salt and sugar in the bowl. Using the dough hook attachment, mix the ingredients together on a low speed. Stir the yeast and water mixture and add to the flour, along with some extra warm water until you have a softish but only slightly sticky dough. Continue kneading the dough with the dough hook for about 5 minutes until it is smooth and elastic. Now add in the olive oil and knead again. It will take a few minutes for this to be incorporated.

Making the dough by hand
If making the dough by hand, place the flour, salt and sugar in a large bowl. Drizzle in the yeast and water and with your hand outstretched like a claw, mix the liquid into

the flour. Add more water as required to bring the dough together into a softish ball. Tip the dough out onto a lightly floured surface and knead for about 5 minutes. Rub in the olive oil (in two or three stages) and knead again until the oil has been incorporated.

Place the dough in a bowl large enough to allow for its expansion. Cover the bowl with clingfilm and leave to rest for at least 1-2 hours or until the dough has doubled in volume. The exact timing will depend on the temperature of the room.

To cut, shape, roll and bake

If using a pizza stone, place it in a cold oven one hour in advance and turn the oven up to its highest setting.

Scoop the dough out onto a lightly floured counter. With a knife or a dough scraper, divide the dough into ten pieces of about 80g each. Place one piece of dough on an unfloured section of the counter. Working with flourless hands, cup your right hand over the dough and using a little downward pressure, move in an anticlockwise direction until the ball of dough becomes a perfectly smooth round. Place each ball on a lightly floured tray and allow to rest for about 15 minutes. If you do not have a pizza stone, preheat a heavy baking tray in the oven for 10 minutes prior to cooking the pittas.

After the resting period, place a ball of dough on a lightly floured counter and roll it out to a thickness of about ½cm or less. Repeat with the remaining dough. Place 2 pittas on a floured paddle and with a quick jerking movement of the wrist, transfer to the pizza stone or the preheated baking tray. Bake until they puff up and are still quite pale - a little hint of colour is fine but no more. Remove from the oven to a wire rack. Repeat with the remaining pittas. While they are still warm, stack the pittas on top of one another in one or two piles and keep covered loosely with tinfoil or clingfilm. If making in advance, rewarm in the oven, wrapped in foil. The pittas are best eaten on the day. Freeze any left over pittas for up to three months.

OVERNIGHT FERMENTATION

If you are having people over for brunch, it is probably best to make the pitta dough the night before. Make the dough as above and leave at room temperature until doubled in volume. Cover the bowl and place in the fridge. The next morning, remove the dough and bring back to room temperature. Shape into balls and then continue as above.

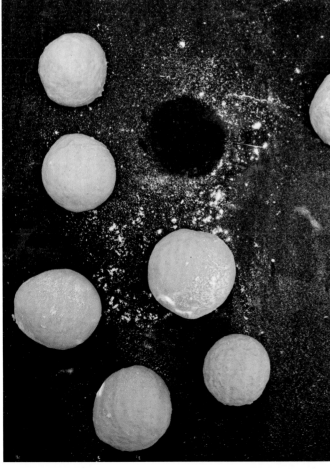

PARISIAN FALAFEL

Makes 28-34 falafel

250g chickpeas, soaked overnight

100g onion, finely chopped

4 cloves garlic, finely chopped

25g parsley, leaves only

25g coriander, leaves and top part of
the stems

2 tbsp ground cumin

2 tbsp ground coriander

1½ tsp salt

1 tsp baking powder

2 tbsp gram flour (use plain if gram
is not available)

sunflower oil, for deep frying

To make the falafel

Place the chickpeas in a bowl and cover them in at least four times the volume of water. Leave them to sit overnight or for at least 8 hours in advance.

Blitz the onion and garlic in a food processor until finely chopped, add the herbs and whizz again. Using a spatula, scrape down the sides of the food processor a couple of times during the process. Drain off all the liquid from the chickpeas and add them to the food processor. Blitz until you have a coarse paste, being careful not to overwork the mixture. Take a knob of the mixture in your palm and squeeze it together to hold a shape. If the mixture does not hold together, blitz again briefly. Tip everything into a bowl and mix in all the remaining ingredients. This can be refrigerated for up to 2 days.

With damp hands, portion the falafel mixture into small balls (about the size of a walnut), pressing the mixture together in your palm. If not using straight away, place on a lined tray and refrigerate, covered, until ready to use.

To cook the falafel

Heat a generous amount of sunflower oil in a wok, saucepan or deep fat fryer. The ideal temperature for deep frying the falafel is 170°C, 325°F or simply test the temperature by dropping a piece of bread into the oil. It should go golden in 10-15 seconds. If the oil is too hot, leave to cool a little before frying.

Line a plate or a tray with kitchen paper and cook the falafel in batches – be careful not to overcrowd the pot as this will lower the temperature of the oil. Have a slotted spoon close to the cooker to remove the falafel quickly. Fry them until they are mahogany brown and drain on kitchen paper. They are best eaten while still hot and will hold for about 20 minutes.

NOTE The oil used in deep frying may be cooled, strained through a very fine mesh strainer and stored in a container for future use. Label and date the container. The oil may be used several times.

PITTA ACCOMPANIMENTS

It is helpful to have a vision of how this works. The tahina sauce is spread thinly on the inside of the pitta followed by some crunchy red cabbage, falafel, perhaps some shallow fried aubergines and one of the pickles. The pitta would usually be served with a tomato sauce along with the yoghurt and mint dressing but I favour using harissa which provides a sharp contrast to the other ingredients. It can get messy but maybe that's the point. If the suggestions that follow are made in advance and lined up in your fridge, this is not so daunting.

Tahina is a sauce made with tahini (which is a purée of sesame seeds), seasoned with lemon juice and garlic and thinned out with a little water. Hunt down an Israeli, Palestinian or Lebanese brand of tahini (available in Asian stores). They are so much more flavoursome and less claggy.

Serves 6

TAHINA
185g tahini
juice of 1-1½ lemons
2 small cloves garlic, crushed
100-150ml water
salt

RED CABBAGE SALAD
300g finely shredded red cabbage
1 tbsp olive oil
1 tbsp lemon juice
a generous pinch of salt

PICKLED CUCUMBER
100g water
100g white wine vinegar
100g sugar
1 cucumber

PICKLED SHALLOT
4-6 small shallots
100ml white wine vinegar
100ml water
100g sugar

Tahina
Place the tahini in a bowl and using a spatula or spoon, beat in the lemon juice. The mixture will seize and become very thick. Add the crushed garlic and the water, one tablespoon at a time, stirring the mixture continuously until it reaches a thick, creamy consistency. Season with a little salt. It will get thicker if refrigerated, so adjust the consistency if necessary.

Red cabbage salad
Mix the ingredients together in a bowl.

Pickled cucumber
Place the water, vinegar and sugar in a saucepan and bring to the boil. Allow to boil for 30 seconds, then turn off the heat and leave the liquid to cool for 10 minutes or longer. Leaving the skin on the cucumber, slice into rounds as thinly as possible and place in a bowl. Pour the pickling liquid over the cucumber. The pickled cucumber will keep in a jar in the fridge for a couple of months.

Pickled shallot
Chop the shallots in half and then very thinly lengthways. Place the white wine vinegar, water and sugar in a small saucepan. Heat, stir to dissolve the sugar and bring to boil for 1-2 minutes. Add the sliced shallot. Bring back to the boil and immediately transfer the liquid and the shallots into a bowl and allow to cool. The shallots will keep for months in the fridge in an airtight jar.

SHALLOW FRIED AUBERGINE
1 aubergine
120ml olive oil
120ml sunflower oil

Shallow fried aubergine

Slice the aubergine in half lengthways, and then slice each half into thin slices, about 3mm thick. Place on a wire rack and salt generously. Leave to sit for about 30 minutes. Put the aubergine slices in a bowl, rinse well and then spread out on a tea towel. Pat dry. If there is any residue of water, they will spit when they hit the oil.

Heat the olive oil and sunflower oil and when hot, add the aubergine. Once the aubergine slices have taken some colour, flip them and repeat on the other side. Remove and keep in a container, covered with a fresh layer of olive oil. They will keep in the fridge for a couple of months. Return them to room temperature before using.

YOGHURT AND MINT DRESSING
400ml yoghurt
1 clove garlic, crushed
pinch salt
4 tbsp extra virgin olive oil
2 tbsp chopped mint
squeeze of lemon juice

Yoghurt and mint dressing

Mix all of the ingredients together.

HARISSA

Harissa is a fiery North African condiment which has so many uses that I always like to have a jar in my fridge. The harissa available in the shops generally offers raw heat but is usually lacking in interest. If you make your own, you can add some tinned piquillo peppers or some home roasted peppers which add a smoky sweetness to balance out the fieriness of the chillies. Combine this with smoked paprika and cumin for a hint of spice and vinegar for an acidic contrast and you have a seasoned heat with serious possibilities.

250g long red chillies
3 garlic cloves
2 heaped tsp cumin seeds, ground
pinch of salt
100g piquillo peppers or
  1 roasted red pepper,
  peeled (see page 20)
2 tsp tomato purée
2 tsp red wine vinegar
4 tbsp olive oil
2 level tsp smoked paprika

Harissa

Slice the top off the chillies, then halve them lengthways. Scrape out and discard the seeds. Blend the chillies in a food processor with the garlic cloves, ground cumin seeds and a pinch of salt until completely smooth. Add the peppers, tomato purée and vinegar and blend again. Transfer to a mixing bowl and stir in the olive oil and paprika. Taste and adjust seasoning.

Spoon into a sterilised jar and pour a film of olive oil over the top. Harissa will keep for several months in the fridge if topped up with a fresh film of olive oil after each use.

PARISIAN PITTA
SPICY RATATOUILLE
TAHINA

Ratatouille is a hearty stuffing for pitta bread. When making ratatouille in the traditional way, aubergines, courgettes and peppers are added to the pot together. In older Parisian bistros it is still often cooked this way, served perhaps with some wild mushrooms or a poached egg on top. More modern versions tend to cook the vegetables separately.

Serves 4

1 red pepper
1 green pepper
1 red onion
salt
olive oil
6 sprigs thyme
1 aubergine
1 medium courgette
2 medium onions, thinly sliced

1 bay leaf
1 dried red chilli
1 tsp tomato paste
1 x 400g tin chopped tomatoes
150ml chicken stock or Marigold
   bouillon
¼ tsp cayenne
¼ tsp smoked paprika
a pinch of dried chilli
   flakes (optional)
squeeze of lemon juice

TO SERVE
tahina (see page 42)
crème fraîche
pitta breads, bought or homemade
   (see page 37)

Preheat oven to 200°C, 180°C fan, 400°F, Gas 6.

Remove the core from the peppers, split in half and scrape out the seeds and membrane. Cut the peppers into rough 5cm x 3cm triangles (the exact size is not important). Slice the red onion in half, and then into 1cm slices. Place the peppers and the red onion on a roasting tray and season with salt. Drizzle over a little olive oil and mix with your hands to coat. Scatter over half the thyme. Cover the tray with tinfoil to stop the vegetables from browning. Place in a preheated oven and roast for about 25 minutes or until the vegetables are tender but still with a slight bite.

At the same time, line a second roasting tray with a silicone mat. Slice the aubergine in half lengthwise and then into slices about 5mm thick. Paint the aubergine slices with olive oil on both sides. Season with salt and place on the mat. Cook on the highest shelf in the oven for about 20-25 minutes or until the aubergines are lightly coloured and completely tender when pierced with the tip of a knife. Half way through the cooking, turn the aubergines over.

Slice the courgette in half lengthways and then in 5mm slices crossways. Heat 2 tablespoons of olive oil in a frying pan and add the courgette. Season with salt and sauté over a high heat, tossing regularly, until the courgette colours a little on the surface but retains a bite. Remove to a bowl.

Heat a medium sized casserole pot. Add 2 tablespoons of olive oil and when hot, add the sliced onions. Season with salt, turn down the heat to low and cook, with a lid on, until the onion is completely tender. Stir regularly during the process. Add the remaining thyme sprigs, bay leaf and dried chilli, cook for a few minutes and then add the tomato paste. Cook out for a minute or two before mixing in the tinned tomatoes. Bring up to the boil and simmer for 5 minutes. Now add the aubergine, red onion, courgette and peppers to the pot, along with the stock, cayenne and smoked paprika. Season with salt and simmer for a further 10-15 minutes until the sauce has reduced. Taste and adjust the seasoning, perhaps adding a pinch of chilli flakes for a bit more kick. Continue cooking for a few more minutes. Remove the dried chilli and discard. Just before serving, add a dash of lemon juice. The ratatouille freezes well.

Warm the pitta bread in tinfoil in the oven. Spread some tahina on the inside of the pitta and spoon the warm ratatouille in the centre. Serve with a spoonful of crème fraîche.

NOTE A hard boiled egg, finely chopped or grated, may be scattered over the top.

PARISIAN PITTA
BEEF BOURGUIGNON
PICKLED SHALLOTS & CRÈME FRAÎCHE

Sometimes you come across an old classic in a new context that gets you to see it in a totally different light. Boeuf bourguignon has lasted the test of time because the combination of beef, wine, lardons of bacon and pearl onions is so stunning. I came across a rich version of the dish, roughly spooned into a pitta with pickled shallots and a blob of crème fraîche at a French food truck. The pickled shallots add a lovely sweetness and cut through the richness of the meat while the crème fraîche on the top melts and oozes over the yielding beef. Utterly delicious. If it's more at the lunch end of brunch, this is the way to serve this old favourite.

Serves 6

25g flour

1.2kg stewing beef, cut into large
  bite size chunks (see note overleaf)

salt

sunflower oil

1 large or 2 medium onions,
  finely chopped

1 medium carrot, finely chopped

2 cloves garlic, crushed

150ml full-bodied red wine

3 small sprigs thyme

1 bay leaf

500ml meat, chicken stock or
  Marigold bouillon

FOR THE GARNISH

300g pearl onions, peeled
  (see overleaf)

10g butter

10g sugar

150g unsmoked bacon lardons

200g chestnut mushrooms

1 sprig thyme

TO SERVE

pitta bread

pickled shallots (see page 42)

crème fraîche

Preheat the oven to 180°C, 160°C fan, 350°F, Gas 4.

Spread the flour in a thinnish layer on a baking tray. Place in the oven and cook for about 5 minutes until the flour turns a sandy colour. Remove from the oven. Browning the flour gives a cleaner taste to the casserole and gets rid of the floury taste.

The beef should be browned in a frying pan in two or three batches. Dry the meat and season with salt. Heat a large frying pan with 2 tablespoons of sunflower oil. Once the oil is hot, add some of the meat in one layer, making sure that the pieces are not too tightly packed together. Sear the meat on a high heat until it caramelises on all sides. Remove to a bowl and continue with the remaining pieces of meat. If there are any burnt bits at the bottom of the pan, wipe out with some kitchen paper. Add another dash of oil to the pan. Add the onion and carrot and cook at a medium heat, tossing regularly until the vegetables soften and turn a pale golden. Mix in the crushed garlic, toss for a minute or so and then return the beef to the pan. Stir in the flour and cook out for a couple more minutes. Deglaze the pan with the red wine and boil for a few minutes. Transfer the beef and vegetables to a casserole pot. Add the thyme and bay leaf and pour in enough stock to barely cover the meat. Bring to the boil, cover with a lid and then transfer to the oven. After about 20 minutes, reduce the temperature to 160°C, 140°C Fan, 320°F, Gas 3 and braise until the meat is meltingly tender, about 2-2½ hours. Timing will vary depending on the cut of meat.

To cook the pearl onions

Place the peeled pearl onions in a saucepan and barely cover with water. Add the butter and sugar and season with salt. Bring to a rapid boil and continue boiling until the water has evaporated and the onions have become caramelised with the residual sugar and butter. If the onions become tender before the water has evaporated, remove them with a slotted spoon, reduce down the onion water by boiling rapidly and then return the onions to the pot towards the end of the cooking. Shake the saucepan to get them evenly coated.

To cook the lardons & the mushrooms

If the mushrooms are very small, leave them whole. If slighter bigger, cut into quarters. Heat a dash of oil in a pan and add the lardons. Sauté at a medium to high heat until the fat renders out and the bacon becomes crisp. Remove from the pan and drain on kitchen paper. Add the mushrooms to the pan (if there is excess fat, drain off some of this beforehand) and toss over a high heat until lightly browned. Season with salt. Stir the mushrooms, lardons and pearl onions into the beef. Check the seasoning.

Spoon the warm beef bourguignon into pitta bread and top with pickled shallots and crème fraîche.

NOTE Buy a stewing cut with a nice marbling of fat. My butcher recommends "ball of the round" (not the "round" which is leaner) for the beef bourguignon which needs to be braised for about 2 to 2 ½ hours or "chuck steak" which will take an hour longer.

THE FASTEST WAY TO PEEL PEARL ONIONS

Trim the pearl onions on both ends, leaving the root end intact, and then throw into boiling water for 2 minutes. Transfer to a bowl of cold water and then remove the skins. They should slide off easily. Very often you need to remove the tough second layer of inner skin as well. If pearl onions are not available, small round shallots (the smaller the better) will do the trick nicely.

MULTISEED BROWN YEAST BREAD

Brown bread coming out of the oven is hard to beat. It gives a sense of accomplishment far out of proportion to the ease with which it is made. This is an unusual recipe as it is so quick to make and does not require a double rising. The treacle gives it a deep malty flavour. You may use one type of seed only or a combination, just so long as it adds up to the total weight required. A very coarse stoneground flour is essential and is not too difficult to find.

sunflower oil, for greasing the tin

2 tbsp treacle

30g fresh yeast or 7g dried yeast

350-425ml warm water,
     about 37°C - 40°C

420g extra coarse stoneground
     wholemeal flour, such as Howard's

40g sunflower seeds

40g pumpkin seeds

10g flaxseeds or linseed

1 rounded tsp salt

EQUIPMENT 900g loaf tin

Preheat the oven to 200°C, 180°C Fan, 400°F, Gas 6.

Grease the inside of the loaf tin very lightly with sunflower oil. Mix the treacle with about 300ml warm water. Crumble in the fresh yeast or if using dried, sprinkle the yeast granules on the surface. Stir and leave for about 5 minutes for the yeast to activate.

Place the flour, seeds and salt in a large mixing bowl and mix together. Have to hand the additional warm water, ready to mix into the bread. Stir the yeast, treacle and water together and pour all at once into the flour. With your hand outstretched like a claw, mix in the liquid, adding in some extra water at the same time until you have a wet, almost sloppy dough (the risk is to make it too dry, in which case it won't rise to the top of the tin).

Scoop the dough into the tin and spread out evenly. It will only come half way up the tin. Leave in a warm place to rise. When the mixture has risen right to the top of the tin - this usually takes about 20-40 minutes - place in the oven for about 45 minutes. Run a knife around the outside edges of the bread, tap the loaf tin upside down on the counter and it should pop out. Return to the oven upside down without the tin for a further 5 minutes. Cool on a wire rack. This bread is definitely best eaten on the day but will hold for longer if there is any left.

RICOTTA PANCAKES
MIXED BERRIES

The ricotta in the batter makes these pancakes moist, light and fluffy and this is further enhanced by the addition of beaten egg whites. If you don't have ricotta to hand, try the buttermilk version below.

Makes about 12 pancakes, about
  10cm in diameter

VANILLA YOGHURT
1 vanilla pod
300g Greek yoghurt
40g honey

FOR THE PANCAKES
120g plain flour
1 tsp baking powder
a pinch of salt
2 tbsp caster sugar
4 eggs, separated
250g ricotta
200ml milk

Mixed berries, such as blueberries,
  raspberries, strawberries, to serve
Maple syrup or agave syrup,
  for drizzling

Split the vanilla pod in half, scrape out the little black seeds and add them to the yoghurt along with the honey. Refrigerate until ready to use.

Place the flour, baking powder, salt and sugar in a large bowl. Using a hand whisk, beat together the egg yolks, ricotta and milk and pour into the bowl with the flour. In a separate bowl, whisk the egg whites until stiff peaks form. Fold the egg whites into the batter just until mixed through.

Heat a non-stick frying pan and add a drizzle of sunflower oil. Spoon a small ladle of mixture per pancake into the pan. Cook until the underside is golden, turn over and repeat on the other side. The pancakes may be wrapped in tinfoil and held in a warm oven if necessary. Serve them with fresh berries and a drizzle of maple or agave syrup. Top with some vanilla yoghurt.

BUTTERMILK PANCAKES

300g plain flour
1 tsp salt
1 tsp baking powder
2 tbsp sugar
60g butter
3 eggs, separated
480ml buttermilk

Mix the flour, salt, baking power and sugar in a bowl. Melt the butter in a small saucepan or in the microwave. Place the whites in a clean bowl and whisk to stiff peaks. Mix the yolks with the buttermilk and whisk into the flour mixture, followed by the melted butter. Finally fold in the egg whites. Cook as above.

BRIOCHE FRENCH TOAST
NECTARINES & BLUEBERRIES

I grew up with "eggy bread" on a Sunday morning. It can be made with any bread but brioche works well for a treat. The choice is to go savoury, eliminate the sugar and opt for bacon and maple syrup or go for this dessert version with whatever fruits are in season.

Serves 6

2 large eggs
70g caster sugar
100g whole milk
1 tsp vanilla extract
10g rum (optional)
40g butter, unsalted
6 thickish slices of brioche

FOR THE FRUIT
3 ripe nectarines (or peaches)
handful of blueberries, fresh
  or frozen
20g castor sugar
crème fraîche, for serving

Preheat the oven to 150°C, 130°C Fan, 300°F, Gas 2.

To cook the French toast
Mix the eggs and sugar in a wide, shallow bowl and using a hand whisk, gradually incorporate the milk and vanilla extract. Add the rum if using.

When ready to cook, heat a frying pan with a knob of butter. Dip two slices of the brioche into the egg mix and turn them over to coat. When the butter is foaming, add the soaked brioche and cook until lightly golden on each side. Place on a tray and keep warm in the oven while you cook the other slices. You will need to wipe out the pan with kitchen paper and add a fresh knob of butter when panfrying each batch.

To cook the fruit
Halve the nectarines and remove the stone. Choose a pan that will hold them in a single layer. Heat the pan and when hot, sprinkle the sugar over the base. When the sugar begins to melt, add the nectarines flesh side down and cook, without moving, until caramelised on the underside. Flip the nectarines over, add a dash of water and continue cooking on a low to medium heat. When the nectarines are warmed through, remove to a plate. Add the blueberries to the pan and, if needed, another dash of water. Simmer for a few minutes until the blueberries release some of their juice. Spoon the fruit over the brioche, along with some of the syrup. Top with a spoonful of crème fraîche.

RASPBERRY BRIOCHE BUNS

A muffin would make a fine finish to a brunch but if you want something that is quite extraordinary, then these brioche buns are worth considering. If you have access to some sort of electric beater, then this is an opportunity to grow your confidence working with yeast. These buns are best suited to weekend baking when you have time to allow them to rise. What makes them particularly worthwhile is the fact that they freeze so well and can be warmed in the oven straight from the freezer.

Makes 19 individual brioche buns

500g plain flour

30g caster sugar

1 tsp salt

1 tsp dried yeast

4 eggs, beaten, at room temperature

120ml milk, room temperature
  or lukewarm

250g butter, at room temperature,
  neither too hard nor too soft,
  cut into 2cm dice

160g frozen raspberries

raspberry jam, for serving

GLAZE

1 egg yolk mixed with a dash
  of cream

EQUIPMENT: 2 x 12 cup muffin tins

Softened butter for greasing the
  inside of the muffin tins

This is a dough best made with a dough hook in a stand mixer. Mix the flour, sugar, salt and yeast together in the mixing bowl and blend together with a dough hook. Beat the eggs and milk together with a fork in a small bowl. With the machine running at medium speed, add the egg mixture slowly to the flour. You should have a soft and slightly sticky dough. (Add an extra dash of milk only if you think the dough is too dry). Continue mixing on speed 1 for about 4 minutes. Add the butter, piece by piece, to the dough while the machine is running. Every couple of minutes, stop the machine and scrape down the sides of the bowl with a spatula. Continue until all the butter has been added and then mix on speed 2 for a further 5 minutes. The dough will be sticky and shiny but there should be no signs of butter.

Cover the bowl with clingfilm and leave at room temperature for about 2 hours until the dough has doubled in bulk. Timing will vary according to the temperature of the room. Judge the dough by how much it has expanded rather than by the time. The dough may be refrigerated at this point for several hours or overnight (see overleaf).

Grease the inside of the muffin tins with some softened butter. (If you have paper muffin holders, it is unnecessary to butter the inside of the tins). Scoop the dough out onto a lightly floured surface. Cut the dough into pieces about 55g in weight. With lightly floured hands, shape roughly and press into the buttered muffin tins (or sit in the paper holders). The dough should come half way up the moulds. Cover with a tea towel and leave to rise for 1½-2 hours until doubled in size. If the buns do not rise sufficiently, they will be not be light enough.

Thirty minutes before cooking, preheat the oven to 200°C, 180°C fan, 400°F, Gas 6 (conventional oven is preferable).

Just before placing in the oven, press 2 frozen raspberries into each bun. (Don't worry, the dough will puff back up again). Mix the egg yolk and cream together and brush on the top of each bun. Place the brioche buns in a preheated oven for about 20 minutes. If the buns are placed on racks at different heights, swop the top and bottom ones towards the end of the cooking. After removing from the oven, leave for a few minutes only, then transfer to a wire rack to cool. They are best served warm with raspberry jam.

These buns freeze well in ziplock bags. They may be reheated from frozen wrapped in foil at 180°C, 160°C Fan, 350°F, Gas 4.

OVERNIGHT FERMENTATION

A slower fermentation improves the quality of the brioche so if it suits, it can work really well to prove the dough overnight. In this case make the dough, leave to rise until almost doubled in size, then cover and refrigerate overnight. The next morning, portion the dough as above and place in the muffin tins. As the dough will be cold from the fridge, the second fermentation will take a little longer, about 2½-3 hours. Once doubled in size, continue as above.

CINNAMON BUNS

There is a deep satisfaction in unfurling a warm sticky cinnamon bun, licking your fingers and relishing every mouthful. I start the process the day before, allow them to rise and then refrigerate them overnight. This makes for an easy triumph on the day.

Makes 12 large buns

175ml milk, lukewarm

1½ tsp / 7g dried yeast

4-5 eggs, room temperature

675g strong flour, or more if required

1½ tsp salt

110g sugar

150g salted butter, at room temp
  neither too hard nor too soft

CARAMEL FILLING & TOPPING

150g butter, soft room temperature

50g dark muscovado sugar

100g soft brown sugar

30ml agave syrup or maple syrup

3 tbsp cinnamon

110g pecans

85g raisins (optional)

GLAZE

1 egg yolk mixed with a dash
  of cream

EQUIPMENT: Baking tin or cast iron
  baking dish 37cm x 26cm (or
  slightly larger) and 7cm deep

To make the dough

Warm the milk until it is lukewarm to the touch (too hot and it will kill the yeast). Place the warm milk in a bowl and sprinkle on the yeast. Stir and leave to sit for about 10 minutes to allow the yeast to dissolve. Crack 4 eggs into a measuring jug and beat with a fork. When the yeast has dissolved, stir and then mix into the eggs.

Place the flour, salt and sugar in the bowl of a stand mixer. Using the dough hook, mix the ingredients together. With the machine running, gradually add the egg and yeast mixture. The dough should become quite soft and sticky by the time all the liquid has been added. If the dough is still a little dry towards the end, beat up another egg and gradually add to the dough. The amount of liquid required will vary with different brands of flour.

Cut the butter into smallish cubes and gradually add piece by piece into the dough. When all the butter has been added, stop the machine and using a spatula, scrape down the sides of the bowl. Continue to mix on speed 2 for a further 5 minutes. The dough will be sticky and shiny but there should be no signs of butter. Scoop the dough out into a widish bowl and seal the bowl tightly with clingfilm. Leave to rise until doubled in bulk, about 2-3 hours. The speed at which the dough will rise will vary according to the temperature of the room. When the dough has doubled, place in the fridge and leave overnight.

Filling and rolling the cinnamon buns

The following morning, prepare the filling. Heat the butter, sugar and agave or maple syrup together until the butter has melted and the sugar dissolves. Pour about one third of the butter and sugar mixture onto the base of the baking dish and spread evenly all over. Whisk the cinnamon into the remaining mixture and allow it to cool (transferring from the saucepan to a jug or bowl means it will cool faster). Chop the pecans into two or three pieces. Set aside with the raisins, if using.

When the filling is cool, but still runny and spreadable, remove the dough from the fridge. Scoop the dough out of the bowl onto a well floured counter top. Roll the dough out into a rectangle about 46cm x 33 cm, keeping the long side nearest the edge of the counter. Pour the filling onto the dough and spread all over with a palate knife. Scatter over the pecans and raisins. Roll the dough into a cylinder. Using a sharp knife, cut the log in half and then each half into 6 buns. Place the 12 buns in the baking dish allowing a little room between each one. Cover the baking dish with clingfilm and leave to rise until doubled in size, probably about 1¾ to 2½ hours.

To cook the buns
Preheat the oven to 180°C, 160°C Fan, 350°F, Gas 4
(a conventional setting is preferable).

When the dough has risen, mix the egg yolk and cream together for the glaze and brush on the top of the buns. Place in the oven. Cook the buns for about 35-40 minutes. The buns will become very brown on the surface by the end. If you remove them too early the dough will not be sufficiently cooked.

Run a knife or spatula around the outside of the tin to loosen the buns. Place a cooling rack over the tin and flip upside down to release them. Allow to cool on the rack. The cinnamon buns are best eaten on the day. They can be rewarmed briefly in the oven, same temperature as above, wrapped in tin foil.

PASTA

PROSCIUTTO & CHERRY TOMATOES LINGUINE	70
TOMATO SAUCE, AUBERGINE & MELTING MOZARELLA RIGATONI	72
CHORIZO, CHERRY TOMATOES & PIQUILLO PEPPERS TROFIE	75
PESTO, GREEN BEANS & BABY POTATOES SPAGHETTI	76
PESTO	78
SALMON, WHITE WINE & DILL SAUCE LINGUINE	79
PEA PUREE, PROSCIUTTO & BROAD BEANS TROFIE	80
SAUTÉED PRAWNS, FENNEL, CHERRY TOMATOES LINGUINE	82
OYSTER & CHESTNUT MUSHROOMS, MADEIRA SAUCE TAGLIATELLE	86
BRAISED LAMB SHANKS, TENDERSTEM BROCCOLI PAPARDELLE	90
BRAISED LAMB MEATBALL SUGO ORECCHIETTE	95
BEEF & PORK RAGÙ TAGLIATELLE	96
DUCK RAGÙ & BABY TURNIPS PAPARDELLE	99

PASTA

I still manage to inveigle my way into kitchens. My most recent foray was in a restaurant called Flour + Water in San Francisco. It was here I ate the best pasta I had ever tasted in my life: a six course pasta tasting menu which was utterly breathtaking. During the course of the evening, I discovered that one of the two owners was Irish. I hastily sent a text to a chef colleague in Dublin who prides himself on the breadth of his contacts and much to my delight, all arrangements had been put in place by the next day.

The morning was spent in the "pasta room". Reyna gave me the warmest of Mexican welcomes and showed me the nettle, squid, porcini and saffron doughs she had already made. What followed were some mesmerising hours as she worked first on her filled shapes - cutting, piping, folding and shaping. Perfectly formed, they were placed on a tray ready for service. We then moved onto the plainer, flatter shapes - tagliatelle, papardelle, stradette and tagliarini – which were tossed in the air and dusted with polenta to ensure that the strands did not stick to one another. I was struck by her rhythm, her quiet focus and the gentle way she used a water spray to mist any pasta that was marginally dry.

Previous page: Duck ragù, baby turnips, papardelle - page 99

In the afternoon, I moved to the main kitchen where the rich aromas of dishes that had been cooking all day were to the fore. These chefs loved their long braises, allowing tastes to develop over a period of hours. I was envious of the boxes of vegetables delivered from nearby farms: bright green peas, fava beans, spring onions, green garlic and asparagus of all sizes and colour. At service, the team moved confidently into their roles. They knew which of the multiple pasta shapes to grab, how to use splashes of the boiling pasta water and whether a little butter, olive oil, herbs or Parmesan would be the required final touch.

This chapter is not suggesting that you should open your own Italian restaurant. It is, however, an opportunity to cook long braises and quick sauces, to try out different pasta shapes, to work out what vegetables can be added, to learn how to use starchy pasta water. It is a chance to work out how best to finish a sauce. This is a gentle invitation to broaden your foundation so that you can move away from too well worn a path. Get some water on the boil!

THINGS YOU SHOULD KNOW ABOUT PASTA

Buying pasta
The recipes in this section are for dried pasta. It's great to make your own, but that is for another day. The great advantage of dried pasta is that it can be sitting there in your cupboard, waiting for you to come home. As with most things, it is worth paying a little more for a better product (of the widely available brands, two of the ones I love the most are Di Cecco and Barilla). Sometimes I favour a durum wheat semolina pasta, sometimes a richer egg-based one, and I like to have a choice of shapes to hand.

Big pot, lots of water
Make sure to cook your pasta in plenty of water. The standard amount is four litres of water for anything up to 400g of pasta. If there is much less water, the pasta may cook unevenly and is more likely to stick together.

Salting the water
There is no salt in commercially prepared pasta. If you do not salt the water adequately, the pasta will taste bland even though you may have a well-seasoned sauce. The standard amount of salt for 4 litres of water is 1½ tablespoons of salt. This might seem like a lot but this is what it takes to season the water for pasta.

Bring the water to a rolling boil
Bring the water to a rolling boil before adding the pasta and then bring it back to the boil as quickly as possible. When the pasta has boiled for a minute or two, separate the pasta with a scoop to prevent it sticking together.

Quantities of pasta per serving
This varies hugely from household to household. The important thing is to assess how many grams of pasta are required for those about to sit down so that you can weigh out the pasta before plopping it in the water. 60g pasta for a starter and 100g for a main course is a commonly quoted recommendation but I often find this too much. I will also base the proportions on how I am serving it. With a meat braise for instance, allow for double the amount of sauce to pasta (or even more). Too much pasta upsets the balance.

Keep it al dente
Pasta should always be al dente which means it should have a slight bite to it. The most common mistake is to overcook pasta. A minute too long and you are heading towards disappointment. Start tasting well in advance of the suggested time to ensure that it does not become overcooked. If you are braising the pasta in the sauce, allow for extra time in the pan.

Retain some pasta water
Once the pasta is ready, it should be drained quickly in a colander. Place a bowl underneath so that you can collect some of the precious water in which the pasta has been cooked. The starchy water adds body to the sauce and ensures that it coats the pasta lightly. It is also invaluable when reheating pasta for second helpings.

Saucing the pasta

There are different ways to sauce pasta. Some sauces, such as pesto, do not benefit from being cooked. In these cases, the sauce is spooned over so that it emulsifies and coats the pasta as it is gently tossed with a little pasta water. More robust sauces are heated and then tossed with the cooked pasta in the pan. At other times the pasta is cooked 80% or 90% of the way and is then simmered in the pan while the sauce continues to reduce to become a perfect consistency to coat the pasta.

Parmigiano Reggiano

Parmigiano Reggiano has a protected European status and is quite simply the best you can buy. It can be aged for 12 months or a number of years. If you buy a piece from a good cheesemonger, it is likely to be more mature, to be sourced from a good cheesemaker and to have a marked difference in complexity. Try to buy a chunk that has been cut directly from the wheel rather than a piece that has been vac-packed. Buy little and often is really the key. As soon as the cheese is cut, it will start to oxidise and over time it loses its aroma and its depth of flavour. The exact amount of Parmesan you require for pasta dishes will vary depending on its intensity. Grate it as you need it and store in cheese paper or tin foil, never in clingfilm. Most pasta dishes benefit from a generous dusting of freshly grated Parmesan, (except in fish dishes where it is omitted altogether). In this chapter, it is often also a key ingredient in finishing the sauce.

Serve swiftly

Pasta needs to be served without delay on hot plates. Should there be a delay, you now know what to do...back to the hob, add a little pasta water and the sauce will be loosened once again.

PROSCIUTTO & CHERRY TOMATOES
LINGUINE

I love a sauce that can be rustled up in the time it takes to cook the pasta. In this recipe the key is good quality prosciutto and sweet, flavourful cherry tomatoes. As the sauce develops, the flavour of the prosciutto perfumes the unsalted butter and this in turn flavours the tomatoes. The nuttiness of the Parmesan adds the final flourish.

If you are merely familiar with supermarket packets of prosciutto, you are in for a glorious surprise when you ask for it to be freshly sliced. The difference in taste and texture is remarkable. Ask for it to be cut only slightly thicker than paper-thin and, if possible, to be layered between wax or cheese paper rather than clingfilm. You will thank yourself with every mouthful.

Serves 4

150g prosciutto slices, sliced
   slightly thicker than paper thin
   (about 8-10 slices)
80g unsalted butter
2 shallots, diced finely
2 red chillies, deseeded and
   finely chopped
400g cherry tomatoes, halved
pinch of dried chilli flakes, optional
400g linguine
15 basil leaves
Parmesan, freshly grated

Bring a large pot of water to the boil. For 4 litres of water, add about 1½ level tablespoons of salt.

Slice the prosciutto crosswise into strips about 1cm in width or less. Cut each slice separately rather than stacking them together. Allow the strips to dry out on the board.

Heat two thirds of the butter in a medium-sized frying pan. Add the shallots and chillies and cook for about 30 seconds. Add the strips of prosciutto, cook gently for about 20 seconds and then add the cherry tomatoes to the pan. Add in a pinch of dried chilli flakes if you wish. Simmer gently to allow the tomatoes to soften.

Meanwhile, put the pasta in the boiling water and cook until al dente. Drain, reserving some of the pasta water and return the pasta to the pot along with the remaining butter. Pour over the prosciutto and tomato mixture and toss together, adding a good splash of pasta water. The water and butter will form an emulsion which will in turn coat the pasta. Chop the basil and mix in along with a fistful or two of Parmesan. The pasta should not look dry and may need another dash of pasta water. Serve sprinkled with extra cheese.

TOMATO SAUCE, AUBERGINE & MELTING MOZZARELLA
RIGATONI

This has been one of my staple tomato sauces for as long as I can remember. I walk in the door after work, grab a frying pan, heat the oil with a few slices of garlic and pour the passata into the pan. I then let the tomato sauce reduce while I wind down. The sauce is transformed by the addition of a ball of milky mozzarella giving it this lovely creamy consistency. You may serve the pasta with some roasted vegetables or panfried chorizo but, in my house, roasted aubergine often wins the day.

Serves 4 - 6

2 aubergines, cut into
  2cm chunks
3 tbsp olive oil
salt

FOR THE TOMATO SAUCE
3 tbsp olive oil
2-3 cloves garlic, thinly
  sliced lengthways
1 jar of tomato passata (750ml) or
  2 x 400g tins tomatoes, puréed
  and sieved
1 tsp sugar
½ tsp chilli flakes
1 tsp fresh oregano or ½ tsp dried
125g fresh mozzarella packed
  in brine, drained
6-8 basil leaves, plus extra
  for garnish
400g rigatoni (or penne)
Parmesan, freshly grated
125g buffalo mozzarella (optional)

Preheat the oven to 220°C, 200°C Fan, 400°F, Gas 4.

To roast the aubergines
Toss the aubergine chunks with olive oil, season with salt and place on a roasting tray. Roast in the oven until completely tender and lightly browned, about 15-20 minutes.

For the tomato sauce
Heat the oil in a frying pan and add the sliced garlic. Cook the garlic for 10-20 seconds until it is just beginning to catch colour at the edges and then add the passata or puréed tomatoes. Mix in the sugar, chilli flakes and oregano and season with salt. Simmer until the tomatoes have reduced to a thickish sauce, about 15 minutes. Chop the fresh mozzarella into rough pieces. Stir into the sauce until it melts and add the basil.

To cook the pasta
Meanwhile, bring a large pot of water to the boil with about 4 litres water and 1½ tablespoons salt. Cook the rigatoni until al dente and then drain, keeping back a little of the pasta water. Place the pasta back in the pot and mix in the tomato sauce, a generous splash of pasta water, one or two fistfuls of grated Parmesan and the aubergine. Transfer to a warmed serving dish and sprinkle with a dusting of Parmesan. Break the buffalo mozzarella into chunks (if using) and scatter over the top. Garnish with some torn basil leaves.

CHORIZO, CHERRY TOMATOES & PIQUILLO PEPPERS TROFIE

I like to keep a tin of piquillo peppers in my cupboard, cherry tomatoes and chorizo in the fridge and a basil plant on my kitchen shelf. With any luck, there will be no shopping required and the cooking time for this recipe will be less than ten minutes. This fits the bill for a quick supper for some hungry mouths.

Serves 4

10 tinned piquillo peppers or 4
   roasted red peppers (see page 20)
15 basil leaves
2 tbsp olive oil
200g chorizo, chopped into
   small dice
1 large red onion, finely chopped
600g cherry tomatoes,
   roughly chopped
½ tsp smoked paprika
¼-½ tsp red chilli flakes
salt
400g trofie or orecchiette pasta
60g-80g freshly grated Parmesan

To make the piquillo pepper sauce

Cut the piquillo peppers into strips. If using roasted peppers, core and deseed the peppers and then cut into strips. Shred the basil leaves. Heat the oil in a medium saucepan and add the diced chorizo. Cook gently until the oil renders out, then add the red onion. Stir to coat with the oil, cover with a lid and allow to soften over a gentle heat for about 10 minutes. Remove the lid, add the cherry tomatoes, smoked paprika and chilli flakes. Season with salt and continue cooking until the tomatoes are softened. Mix in the strips of pepper and basil. Cook for a few more minutes to develop the flavours.

To cook the pasta

Fill a large pot with about 4 litres water and add 1½ tablespoons of salt. Bring to a rolling boil and add the pasta. After a couple of minutes, stir to separate the trofie. Cook until al dente. Drain, reserving some of the pasta water. Pour the pasta into the sauce along with a dash of pasta water and simmer for a couple of minutes. Add Parmesan to taste.

PESTO, GREEN BEANS & BABY POTATOES
SPAGHETTI

We think of ourselves as a potato nation but the Italians are no slouches when it comes to spuds. They even love potatoes on their pizza so it is not surprising that they also serve them with pasta. You will find this verdant dish on the menu of every trattoria in Genoa and right down the northwest coastline of Italy. You can make it by hand (see overleaf) but it is also possible to buy good quality pesto. Judge it firstly by the colour – if it is the same vibrant green as basil itself, it is worth checking out.

Serves 4-5 people

10 smallish baby potatoes
300g French beans, topped
   and tailed
400g spaghetti
8 tbsp pesto (see overleaf)
salt
freshly grated Parmesan

To prepare the vegetables

Boil the potatoes in their skins until tender but still firm. Remove to the chopping board and cut in halves or quarters. Bring a large pot of water to the boil with about 4 litres water and 1½ tablespoons salt. Blanch the green beans for no more than two minutes in the boiling pasta water. Scoop them out and refresh in cold water. Drain the beans after a couple of minutes.

To finish

Return the water to a rolling boil and add the spaghetti. After a couple of minutes, stir with a pasta scoop to separate the strands. In the last minute of cooking, add the potato and green beans back into the water. When the pasta is al dente, drain, holding back some of the pasta water. Place the pesto in the bottom of the pot, along with a few tablespoons of pasta water. Add the spaghetti, potato and green beans, adding more pasta water as necessary and toss until the pesto loosely coats the spaghetti. Serve with a grating of Parmesan.

NOTE Other suitable shapes for pasta with pesto are tagliatelle, fettuccine, linguine and trofie.

PESTO

A long time ago, when pesto started appearing on our shelves, I used to wonder what all the fuss was about. It was good but not memorable. Then I went to work in Liguria, the spiritual home of pesto. On my very first day in a busy kitchen, I presumed that the vast quantities of pesto would have to be made in a food processor. Instead, I was given a giant pestle and mortar and handed huge bunches of their small-leafed basil and grassy Ligurian olive oil. The chef proudly told me that their basil was not just one of their prized ingredients but that it had a DOP label, in other words it had a protected European status. I was blown away by the result. I sometimes take the shortcut of whizzing the basil in a food processor but when I return to making my pesto by hand, I wonder why I had ever strayed.

1 clove garlic, crushed
coarse sea salt
30g pine nuts
60g basil leaves
50g Parmesan, grated
about 120ml extra virgin olive oil,
    preferably Ligurian

Using a pestle and mortar

Place the garlic, salt and pinenuts in a large mortar and crush it with the pestle until smooth. Add the basil to the mortar a little at a time and continue pounding, adding another pinch of salt to help the process. When all the basil has broken down, stir in the Parmesan and the olive oil.

Using a food processor

Crush the garlic and add to the food processor along with the pinenuts and Parmesan. Blend briefly to crush the nuts to a coarse paste. Add in the basil and whizz for a few seconds. Remove the lid and scrape down the sides of the food processor before whizzing again briefly. Add salt and while the motor is running, pour in enough olive oil to form a stiff paste. Do not over-process or the basil will become tired. Scoop into a bowl and add more olive oil as required. Taste and add another pinch of salt if necessary.

To store in the fridge, fill the pesto into a sterilised jar. Cover with a thin layer of olive oil. Seal the jar tightly. The pesto will keep for several weeks but is best eaten within the first few days. Be sure to use a clean spoon every time you dip into it, wipe down the sides of the jar and cover with a fresh layer of olive oil. This will help prolong its shelf life. Seal the jar and keep refrigerated.

SALMON IN A WHITE WINE & DILL SAUCE
LINGUINE

When I started giving classes from my home kitchen, the same core group used to come for a whole season of evening courses. I was kept on my toes coming up with new material. One of the students asked me for dinner one night and gave me a wonderful pasta dish with salmon and dill in a fish "velouté" sauce. When I asked her for the recipe, she pulled out a printed copy. I creased up laughing as it was one of my own from the previous year. How different it tasted with a glass of white wine in my hand and having someone else cook it. If you give it a go, don't hesitate to issue me an invitation. I'll bring the wine!

Serves 4

175ml dry white wine
1 shallot, finely chopped
3 cracked black peppercorns
4 dill stems
1 bay leaf

200ml fish stock, chicken stock or
　Marigold bouillon
250ml cream
2 tbsp chopped dill, plus extra
　for serving
good squeeze lemon juice

800g salmon
1 tbsp olive oil, for cooking
　the salmon
75ml "Noilly Prat"* or other dry
　vermouth (optional)
280g tagliatelle
a generous knob of unsalted butter,
　for tossing with the pasta

*Noilly Prat is a brand of French vermouth used extensively in fish sauces. It can also be used as a replacement for white wine in risottos.

Place the first five ingredients in a saucepan and boil to reduce to about 3 tablespoons. Remove the dill stems and bay leaf and discard. Add in the stock, boil to reduce by half, then pour in the cream and reduce again by about a quarter. Season, add a squeeze of lemon juice and the chopped dill. This white wine sauce can be made in advance and refrigerated.

Remove the skin and any small bones from the salmon. Dry with kitchen paper. Cut the fish into large bite-sized cubes. Heat the olive oil in a non-stick frying pan and when hot, add the salmon. Season with salt, sear for a couple of minutes and then deglaze the pan with the Noilly Prat. Boil for 30 seconds before pouring in the white wine sauce. Turn the pieces over in the sauce and simmer gently for a few minutes.

Meanwhile, bring a large saucepan of water to the boil. For 4 litres of water, add 1½ tablespoons of salt. Cook the pasta until al dente. Drain, keeping back some of the pasta water. Return the pasta to the pot, add a good knob of butter and a generous dash of pasta water. Pour about half of the sauce from the pan into the pasta and simmer for a minute or so.

Scoop the pasta onto each plate and spoon over the remaining sauce along with the chunks of salmon. Sprinkle with some extra chopped dill and serve immediately.

NOTE　Monkfish works very well as an alternative to salmon. Scallops may also be caramelised in the pan (see page 180) and served alongside.

PEA PURÉE, PROSCIUTTO & BROAD BEANS
TROFIE

It's funny how often we get drawn to tomatoes as the starting point for pasta dishes. A great way to break out of this mould is with this pea purée. It is not only a very fresh, light taste but it is an alluringly vivid colour. It is a perfect base for so many other ingredients. Trofie is a short, twisted, delicate pasta often served with pesto and so is well suited to this dish.

Serves 4

360g peas, fresh or frozen
1 tbsp cream (or full fat milk)
sea salt
50ml water, or more as required

300g broad beans, fresh or frozen
60g prosciutto
3 spring onions

400g trofie (or penne)

2 tbsp olive oil
2 cloves garlic, finely diced
120ml chicken or vegetable stock
zest of half lemon
30g unsalted butter
freshly grated Parmesan, for serving
good squeeze of lemon juice
handful of pea shoots, if available

Cook the peas in boiling salted water for about 2 minutes. Remove to a bowl of ice cold water. Leave for a couple of minutes and then drain. Place in a blender with the cream, salt and water and whizz until perfectly smooth. Taste and adjust seasoning as required.

Blanch the broad beans in boiling salted water for about 2 minutes, then place in a bowl of cold water and drain when cold. Press the beans out of their shells to reveal the tender green bean within. Discard the shells. Slice the prosciutto into thin strips about ½cm thick. Chop the spring onions into thinnish rounds.

To prepare the other ingredients
Bring a casserole pot with about 4 litres of water and 1½ tablespoons of salt to the boil. Add the pasta to the boiling water, stir and bring back to the boil. Cook the pasta until al dente, then drain, holding back some of the pasta water.

Meanwhile, heat a frying pan and pour in the olive oil. When hot, add in the strips of prosciutto. They will sizzle and go a shade darker. After about 1 minute, add in the chopped garlic, along with the spring onions. Cook for a couple of minutes and then pour in the stock. Bring up to the boil and reduce for a couple of minutes. Add the broad beans to the pan along with the stock. Heat and then throw in the trofie. Mix in the pea purée, lemon zest and butter and swirl the pan to incorporate the ingredients. If the sauce is a little thick, add a few tablespoons of pasta water and continue simmering until the sauce coats the pasta loosely. Add a squeeze of lemon juice and taste for balance and seasoning.

Garnish with grated Parmesan. Scatter over the pea shoots, if using.

NOTE The broad beans may be replaced by blanched asparagus, peas or sautéed courgettes.

SAUTÉED PRAWNS, FENNEL
CHERRY TOMATOES
LINGUINE

Prawns can be sweet, delicious and succulent but they are not the star of the show here. If you are not used to fennel, this is the moment of conversion. Seafood and fennel have a natural affinity, particularly with a drop of Pernod which underlines the anise flavour of this underrated vegetable. The magic of this dish is having really crunchy fennel to provide a contrast in texture to the pasta.

Serves 4

24 tiger prawns, peeled,
  without heads
2 fennel bulbs

olive oil for frying
salt
2 small shallots, finely sliced
2 cloves garlic, thinly sliced
60ml Pernod (or 75ml dry vermouth
  such as "Noilly Prat" or white wine)
15-20 ripe cherry tomatoes, halved
pinch chilli flakes
60g Ligurian black olives or Greek
  Kalamata, optional
a small handful flat leafed
  parsley, chopped
lemon juice, to taste

200g linguine
2 tbsp olive oil
40g Parmesan

To prepare the prawns

Dry the prawns with kitchen paper. With a small knife, cut a little slit down the back of each one and, with the point of a knife, remove the intestinal tract. Cut off the stalks from the fennel and discard. Slice the fennel into quarters, remove the core and then slice lengthways, about 2-4mm thick.

To pan fry the prawns & fennel

Heat a non-stick frying pan and add 2 tablespoons of olive oil. When hot, add half the prawns (unless you have a really large frying pan), season with salt and sear on a medium high heat until the prawns pick up a bit of colour on the underside. Turn them over and sear again for a further minute or two. The exact timing of the prawns will vary depending on their size. Remove them to a tray. Dry out the pan, if necessary, with a piece of kitchen paper. Repeat the process with the remainder of the prawns. Wipe out the pan.

Pour 2 tablespoons of olive oil into the frying pan. Add the shallots and cook for about 30 seconds, stirring regularly and then mix in the fennel slices. Season and cook for about 4-5 minutes at a medium heat, stirring regularly. The fennel will pick up a little colour as you go but should still be very crunchy, even at the end. Once the fennel is lightly caramelised (it will not be evenly so), add the garlic to the pan for a minute. Deglaze the pan with the Pernod (or use vermouth or white wine) and then mix in the cherry tomatoes, chilli flakes and olives (if using). Cook for a few minutes to allow the tomatoes to soften a little. Return the prawns to the pan and reheat. Add a good squeeze of lemon juice and the chopped parsley.

To cook the pasta

Meanwhile, bring a pot of water to the boil with about 4 litres of water and 1½ tablespoons salt. Add the linguine to the pot and cook until al dente. Drain the pasta, holding onto some of the pasta water. Return the pasta to the pot, drizzle over some extra virgin olive oil and add a good splash of pasta water. Mix in the Parmesan and toss together. Place the pasta on the plate and top with the prawn and fennel sauté.

ON GLUTEN

At the cookery school we try to be sensitive to the requirements of coeliacs and to respect their hypersensitivity to gluten. Ireland has one of the highest rates (about 1% of the population) of this largely hereditary and incurable disease. What is puzzling, however, is the wildly increasing number of people who are reporting a gluten intolerance. The most recent estimate is that up to a third of the population now avoid or would choose to avoid gluten and yet studies show that a tiny fraction of this number (less than 3%) have any reaction at all when objectively tested. It is a bewildering statistic.

My hunch is that there are two factors at play, one very ancient and one much more recent. The ancient angle regards the way the human brain processes threat differently to other mammals. If a group of antelope are hunted down and one is attacked, the herd quickly return to grazing minutes later without a backward glance. Our threat system, in comparison, is much more reactive. Once any threat is identified our whole system responds, we remain on alert for much longer periods and we are motivated to avoid this threat in the future. While this vigilance to threat was a helpful capacity for our predecessors, it is not so helpful now. This ancient system now clashes with the more recent phenomenon that we are inundated with threat messages. Fear has infiltrated every aspect of our lives and this is particularly evident in the area of food. Perhaps this explains what happens when we are bombarded by the links between gluten and ill-health. If we hear that gluten may not do us good, we will tend to log the information without working out whether it came from a respected health institute or a faddish (if beautiful) actress or model. Our brain merely sends an urge to avoid any gluten intake so as to calm our ancient threat system. The more frequently we avoid, the stronger the pathway becomes. As time goes on, it feels safer to avoid anything with gluten.

We need to work out how to avoid getting caught up in this frenzy. An important step in this battle is to appreciate what is going on. The food industry has realised that they can trade on our worries. There is no faster growing area than the "made without ..." sector flagging some demonised ingredient like gluten that is omitted from a food product with much fanfare. We need to reflect on these messages. It would be a medical phenomenon of unheard of proportions if the population were actually developing intolerances to gluten at the rate of current avoidance.

Our goal should be to keep some perspective. Read the actual science rather than any claims that "research shows" this or that. Remember that if something like gluten has been taken out of a product, something much worse is likely to have been put in. Start seeing a health claim on a product as a good reason to pass it by. At least fresh food comes with no message at all. Perhaps that is the easiest way to get back to your innate wisdom about what is good for you.

OYSTER & CHESTNUT MUSHROOMS
MADEIRA SAUCE
TAGLIATELLE

Strange things happen when you live in foreign cities. Many years ago I lived in a basement flat in Vancouver with my husband, Richard. One evening there was a knock at the door and there was a man with a wide flat basket filled to the brim with orange chanterelle mushrooms. He explained that he was over from one of the nearby islands, selling door to door. I couldn't believe my luck and gleefully scooped up handfuls. I lived there for three mushroom seasons and he always included me on his visits. I used them in different ways but my favourite was to toss them with a hint of garlic, thyme, madeira, a bit of stock and cream and serve them over pasta. His visits were reason enough to look forward to the Fall season. You may not be able to find wild mushrooms but you can still rustle up a great pasta dish with farmed oyster, shitake, or chestnut mushrooms which are available all year round - and if the doorbell rings, you never know who could be there.

Serves 4

225g oyster mushrooms
225g chestnut mushrooms
4 small sprigs thyme
olive oil, for cooking
2 cloves garlic, crushed
2 large shallots, finely chopped
4 tbsp Madeira, medium dry
150ml chicken, vegetable stock
  or Marigold bouillon
200ml cream
bunch of chives
320g tagliatelle
freshly grated Parmesan

Cut the oyster mushrooms in half if they are large. Slice the chestnut mushrooms finely. Pull the thyme leaves off the stalks and chop roughly.

To prepare the sauce
Heat a large frying pan and then add a dash of olive oil. Sauté the mushrooms in batches over a high heat, tossing continuously until they begin to wilt. Towards the end of the cooking, add a sliver of crushed garlic, seasoning and thyme. Wipe out the pan with kitchen paper, if necessary, and repeat with the remaining mushrooms. Remove from the pan.

Heat the pan with another dash of oil and add the chopped shallots. Cook for a minute or so and then return the mushrooms to the pan. Toss together and pour in the Madeira. Allow to boil for 20 seconds or until reduced by half. Add the stock and cream and simmer gently for about 5 minutes to allow the cream to become infused with the mushroom flavours. Be careful not to allow the sauce to become too thick. Taste to check the seasoning and sprinkle in the chives.

To cook the pasta
Meanwhile, bring a large pot of salted water to the boil (about 4 litres of water and 1½ tablespoons of salt). Add the pasta, bring back to the boil and stir with a pasta scoop. Simmer until al dente and then drain, reserving some of the pasta water. Scoop the pasta into

the pan, along with a small ladleful of pasta water and toss together over the heat. Mix in a couple of fistfuls of Parmesan and toss to mix. If the sauce is becoming too dry, add another dash of pasta water. Serve immediately with an extra dusting of cheese.

SEASONAL VARIATION

When in season, other mushrooms to hunt down are the jet black Trompettes de Mort. They are quite delicate and wilt quickly in the pan but their flavour is intense.

With the odd exception, I generally never dunk any wild mushrooms in water. It is best to use a pastry brush to remove the excess dirt or wipe them with damp kitchen paper.

DEEP-BRAISING SAUCES

"Braise" is a great word – a stew or even casserole does not have the same ring. On a wintry Sunday, I love to put a pot in the oven for a few hours, so the meal is evolving while I attend to other things. Whereas previously I might have made a braise for a single meal, I would now always cook more than required and squirrel away meal-sized portions in the freezer to be served up with pasta on any night of the week. I like to have lots of sauce so that it has pride of place rather than merely coating the pasta. It is also an excuse to blanch a seasonal vegetable (baby carrots, tender stem broccoli or baby turnips, for example) and add them to the pan during the final stage of cooking. These deep, intense meaty sauces are truly heart-warming on a cold evening.

Braises can be cooked quickly with more tender cuts of meat but this would miss the point. They work best for a less tender cut that would be tough if cooked quickly but will be succulent if simmered gently over a longer time. There are two essential additions. Firstly, there are the "aromatics" which would usually include vegetables (carrots, celery, onions), some hard herbs (rosemary, thyme, bay leaves) and perhaps pancetta or bacon. The second addition is a liquid (which could be water, stock, wine or beer). Now build up a picture of what is happening under the lid. The simmering liquid vaporises into a steam that cooks the meat and vegetables, which in turn release their juices into the liquid. As the cooking progresses, the broth concentrates in flavour as it continues to simmer.

In the following section, there are four examples of "braises" all of which could be served in other ways (such as with mashed potatoes or rice) but have been chosen because they can become outstanding ragù sauces to serve with pasta.

BRAISED LAMB SHANKS
TENDER STEM BROCCOLI
PAPARDELLE

This is a very slow braise which yields a big bold sauce, further deepened with the addition of dried porcini mushrooms. Shanks require long slow cooking but all the time when they are bubbling quietly away in the oven, the flavours are becoming richer and more intense. The tender stem broccoli may be replaced by another vegetable.

Serves 4

12g dried porcini mushrooms
olive oil, for cooking
4-6 lamb shanks
salt
1 large onion, finely diced
1 stick celery, finely diced
1 large carrot, finely diced
2 bay leaves
1 tbsp tomato purée
200ml white wine
1 x 400g tin chopped tomatoes
1 small sprig rosemary (or use
   3 sprigs of thyme instead)
500ml lamb, beef, veal or
   chicken stock

250g tender stem broccoli

320g papardelle
60g unsalted butter
freshly grated Parmesan, about 80g

Soaking the dried porcini
Place the dried porcini in a small jug and pour over 150ml boiling water. Leave to sit for about 15 minutes. Any grit on the mushrooms will sink to the bottom so when draining off the liquid, leave behind any residue. Reserve the liquid and chop the mushrooms finely.

To prepare the lamb shanks
Heat a large frying pan with a couple of tablespoons of olive oil. Add the lamb shanks, season with salt and brown slowly on a medium heat, for about 15 minutes, until golden brown all over. At the same time, heat a dash of oil in a casserole pot and add the onions. Season with salt and then cover with a lid. Turn down the heat to low and cook slowly to soften the onions, about 10 minutes. Add the celery, carrots and bay leaves and continue cooking gently with the lid on. When the vegetables have softened, remove the lid and stir in the tomato purée. Transfer the lamb shanks to the casserole and deglaze the lamb shank pan with the white wine, scraping up any crusty bits at the bottom. Pour the white wine into the casserole pot and boil to reduce by about half. Add the dried porcini, porcini water, tinned tomatoes and rosemary. Pour in enough stock to barely cover the shanks. Bring back to the boil, cover with a lid and transfer to a preheated oven. Braise for about 3-4 hours or until the meat is meltingly tender. If you are making the braise in advance, then allow to cool and refrigerate. Any fat will solidify on the top and may be removed easily. If eating straight away, allow the sauce to settle. Degrease any fat which rises to the top. Taste and adjust the seasoning.

Remove the lamb shanks from the sauce. Pull the meat off the bone, leaving it in chunks. Check for sinewy or fatty pieces and discard these. Return the meat to the sauce.

To prepare the broccoli

Trim off any coarse-looking leaves or tough ends of the stalk. Shave the stalk ends with a peeler if they are thick. Blanch the broccoli in boiling salted water until tender but still with a bite. Refresh in cold water unless using straight away and drain.

To prepare the pasta

Bring a large pot of water to the boil with about 4 litres of water and 1½ tablespoons of salt. Add the papardelle. Place the lamb and sauce in a deep frying pan and heat gently. When the pasta is about 90% cooked, drain, reserving the pasta water. Add a generous dash of pasta water to the pan, along with the butter. Bring to simmering point and add the cooked pasta. Continue cooking until the sauce reduces and coats the pasta. Pour some pasta water into the pot if the sauce thickens too quickly. Towards the end of the cooking, mix in the broccoli and allow to warm through. Add in a fistful of Parmesan. Toss to coat and serve immediately, along with an extra sprinkling of cheese.

BRAISED SHOULDER OF LAMB

If you don't have time to cook the lamb shanks, then adapt the recipe using a braised shoulder of lamb. Follow the basic method as above, browning the pieces of lamb in a few batches and add them to the casserole with the aromatics. Reduce the tomato purée to 1 teaspoon and the tinned tomatoes to 200ml. The amount of stock required will be considerably less, say perhaps 300ml, or enough to barely cover the lamb. At the end of the cooking if the sauce is too runny, reduce it down by boiling to concentrate the flavour but remember you do need a decent amount of sauce. The total cooking time will be about 1½ hours.

You can buy cubed shoulder of lamb at a butcher. I prefer to cut it up myself as I can keep the pieces chunkier and take more care to remove the excess fat. Ask for 1kg boned forequarter of lamb. Once trimmed it will yield 700g cubed lamb, enough to serve 4 people.

BRAISED LAMB MEATBALL SUGO
ORECCHIETTE

This is a relatively quick braise but it is still important that the meat is not too lean or it will become dry as it cooks. I always go to my butcher so that I can choose meat that is marbled with fat as it will taste sweeter and be more succulent. I will also use the favoured secret of the Italian mammas and add bread soaked in some milk because there is no better way of keeping the meatballs soft and moist.

If you are in the mood for a more exotic shape of pasta, then the small dome-shaped orecchiette is perfect for scooping up this sauce (or sugo). Homely, satisfying and begging for a glass of wine.

Serves 4-5

MEATBALLS

100ml milk

50g white bread, such as ciabatta, broken into chunks

500g lamb mince (from the shoulder)

300g pork mince (preferably from the belly)

3 garlic cloves, crushed

½ teaspoon salt

1 tbsp dried oregano

½ tsp ground black pepper

1½ tsp fennel seed, ground (see note)

FOR THE SAUCE

2 tbsp olive oil

1 large onion, very finely diced

2 small carrots, very finely diced

2 stalks celery, very finely diced

3-4 tbsp tomato purée

500ml chicken stock or Marigold bouillon

1 bay leaf

400g orecchiette pasta

30g unsalted butter

50g Parmesan, freshly grated plus extra for serving

To make the meatballs & sauce

Pour the milk over the bread in a bowl and leave it to soften. Mix all the minced meat ingredients together. Squeeze the excess milk from the bread and add to the meat, breaking it into crumbs as best you can. Mix well.

Heat the oil in a deep frying pan. Break off small clumps of the mince (about the size of a large marble), add to the pan and sear, turning occasionally, so that they are browned all over. (The meatballs may need to be browned in two batches). Remove from the pan and set aside. Add the onion, carrot and celery and cook for about 5-10 minutes with a lid on, until the vegetables begin to soften. Mix in the tomato purée. Stir everything together and add the chicken stock and bay leaf. Return the meatballs to the pan. Simmer gently until the stock has reduced by half which will take about 30 minutes.

To cook the pasta

Bring a large pot of water to the boil. For 4 litres of water, add about 1½ level tablespoons of salt. Add the orecchiette to the pot. Meanwhile, heat the sauce in a deep frying pan and swirl in the butter. When the pasta is 90% cooked, drain, holding back some of the pasta water. Add a small ladleful of pasta water to the sauce, followed by the orecchiette and toss together. Simmer for a few minutes, reducing the sauce to coat the pasta. Add a fistful of Parmesan and another dash of pasta water if necessary to keep it loose. Serve with extra Parmesan.

NOTE   If you don't have fennel seeds, replace with 60g grated Parmesan

BEEF & PORK RAGÙ
TAGLIATELLE

From my earliest days I strove to move away from the uniform Bolognese sauce that was ubiquitous. A change that made real impact was to include milk. I first saw this in Italy where I was surprised how half a litre of milk could give such a sweet creaminess to the sauce. A second common change was to omit the much-favoured tins of tomatoes and put in just a small amount of tomato purée. This allows the meat to take centre stage. The final result is a hearty, warming sauce ready to coat flat strands of pasta.

Serves 4

2 tbsp olive oil, plus extra
   as required
2 small onions, finely diced
salt
2 carrots, finely diced
2 celery stalks, finely diced
100g unsmoked streaky
   bacon lardons
450g beef mince
225g pork mince
2 tbsp tomato purée
120ml white wine
2 bay leaves
2 small sprigs rosemary
600ml chicken stock or
   Marigold bouillon
250ml full fat milk

320g tagliatelle
20g unsalted butter
freshly grated Parmesan

To prepare the ragù

Heat the oil in a large casserole pot. When hot, add the finely diced onion. Stir, season with salt, cover with a lid and turn down the heat to low. Allow to sweat, stirring regularly, until the onion has become translucent and is completely tender. This process will take about 10 minutes. Add the finely diced carrot and celery to the pot, stir to mix and continue cooking for a further 5 minutes to soften the vegetables.

Increase the heat and mix in the bacon lardons. Sauté over a medium heat until the fat renders out and the bacon becomes lightly coloured. Increase the heat to high and add in the beef and pork mince. Brown the meat, stirring regularly until the meat loses its pink colour. Season, stir in the tomato purée and then pour in the white wine. Boil the wine until it has reduced almost to a glaze. Add the bay leaves, rosemary sprigs and stock, bring up to the boil and then turn down the heat to the very gentlest simmer. Allow to cook for about an hour or until reduced by at least half. Bring the milk to a simmer and add to the meat. Cover the sauce with a lid, leaving it slightly ajar, and continue cooking for a further 30 minutes or so at a gentle bubble, adding more stock if the ragù becomes too dry. Remove the bay leaves, the sprigs of rosemary (or the rosemary needles if they have fallen off) and discard. The sauce will keep in the fridge for 3 or 4 days or for a number of months in the freezer.

To prepare the pasta

Bring a large pot of pasta water with about 4 litres of water to the boil. Add 1½ tablespoon salt and return to the boil. When the tagliatelle is cooked about 90% through, drain, holding back some of the pasta water. Meanwhile, heat the ragù in a frying pan and bring to a

gentle simmer. Add the butter and swirl to combine. Add in a good dash of pasta water and the pasta. Simmer until the sauce coats the pasta loosely. Towards the end, mix in a fistful of Parmesan and grate some more to bring to the table.

DUCK RAGÙ, BABY TURNIPS
PAPARDELLE

I remember overhearing my butcher's response to someone asking what cuts are best for a braise. "Near the hoof or near the horn" was his reply! He obviously wasn't thinking of a duck at the time but the same principle applies: duck breast would be unsuitable and duck legs would be ideal. This recipe is the first in this section to use red wine to enrich the liquid. If they are in season, I will add a root vegetable such as baby turnips (sometimes found under their French name, "navets") which are roasted until tender and then added to the pan towards the end of the cooking. Roasted celeriac, butternut squash or braised baby carrots would be great alternatives.

Serves 4

5g dried porcini

4 duck legs with thighs
salt
2 tsp chopped thyme leaves
freshly ground black pepper

1 large onion, finely diced
1 carrot, finely diced
1 celery stalk, finely diced
2 bay leaves
6 sage leaves
1 tbsp tomato purée
180ml full-bodied red wine
300ml beef, veal, duck, chicken
   stock or Marigold Bouillon

320g papardelle
30g unsalted butter
freshly grated Parmesan

roasted baby turnips (see overleaf)

See photo page 63

Preheat the oven to 180°C, 160°C fan, 350°F, Gas 4.

Soaking the dried porcini
Place the dried porcini in a small jug and pour over 150ml boiling water. Leave to sit for about 15 minutes. Any grit on the mushrooms will sink to the bottom so when draining off the liquid, leave behind any residue. Reserve the liquid and chop the mushrooms finely.

Braising the duck legs
Trim the excess skin and fat off the duck leg, leaving enough skin to extend slightly beyond the flesh of the leg. Sprinkle the legs with some sea salt, thyme and black pepper. Heat a frying pan till warm and add the duck legs to the pan, skin side down. It is not necessary to add any oil to the pan as the fat will automatically render from the duck. Cook the duck legs slowly on the skin side for about 10 or 15 minutes. If there is excess fat in the pan, drain the duck fat and set aside for another use (such as roasting potatoes). When the skin is a rich golden brown colour, remove the duck legs from the pan.

Pour out all but 2 tablespoons of duck fat from the pan. Add the onions, carrots, celery, bay leaves and sage and stir to scrape up any crusty bits from the bottom of the pan. Season with salt, cover with a lid and soften over a low heat for about 10 minutes, stirring regularly. Mix in the tomato purée and then deglaze the pan with the red wine. Bring to the boil and keep it bubbling to reduce by about half. Arrange the duck legs in a single layer in the pan, skin side up, and pour in enough stock so that they are barely covered. (If the pan is not ovenproof, transfer to a casserole). Bring to the boil and then transfer to the oven. Check the duck legs after an hour but they will probably take another 30 minutes. If the sauce is becoming too dry, add a little more stock. When the meat comes easily away from the bone, it is ready. Allow the sauce to settle and degrease any fat which comes to the top. If you make the braise in advance, cool, refrigerate and remove the fat at a later point. If the sauce is still quite thin, remove the duck legs and reduce the sauce to concentrate the flavour. At the very end, correct the seasoning.

Transfer the duck legs to a chopping board. Remove the skin and discard. Pick the duck meat off the bone, leaving it in large chunks. Add the duck meat back to the sauce.

To finish the pasta

Bring a large pot of water to the boil. For 4 litres of water, add 1½ level tablespoons of salt. Meanwhile, warm the duck and its sauce in a deep frying pan with the butter. Add in the roasted baby turnips, if using. When the pasta is 90% cooked, drain, keeping back a bowl of pasta water. Pour a good splash of pasta water into the sauce, add the pasta to the pan and simmer for a few minutes until the sauce reduces and coats the strands of papardelle. Add in a fistful of grated Parmesan and toss to emulsify. Serve immediately. Finish with a dusting of Parmesan.

ROASTED BABY TURNIPS

12 baby turnips or less
  depending on size
olive oil
knob of butter

Turnips can vary dramatically in size. If they are tiny, slice them in half, leaving some of the stalks on for show. If they are larger, like the size of a medium beetroot, remove the stalk and cut them into wedges. Heat the oil in a frying pan. Add the turnips in a single layer and colour lightly in the pan. Season with salt, add a knob of butter and toss together. Transfer to a preheated oven until tender. These can be added to the duck sauce along with the pasta in the final stage of cooking.

VEGETABLES

VEGETABLES

I feel I am a more thoughtful cook when I am preparing dishes without meat. I am more aware of combinations, textures and balance. It challenges me to be more inventive in the kitchen. It's a little more stimulating than saying I am going to begin with a piece of chicken and then move unthinkingly to the usual accompaniments. With vegetables I am more aware of seasonality. I know this word is trotted out easily but it is still too often overlooked. What are the local, freshest vegetables available to me? This is a question to inform the appetite. I address my stock of couscous, rice, bulgur and see what jumps out, because there are times I really do crave something and times I don't. My next port of call is the top shelf of my fridge. I have my own personal word for what lies up there. These are some of my "elevators". An elevator is a component that lifts a dish out of the ordinary. I could make some couscous and throw in a few grilled vegetables; I could pull together some greens for a salad; I could put some vegetables in a pastry and put them in the oven. These are all fine but I want something beyond fine. I want something to get me salivating in anticipation. I want something that will elevate the experience. An elevator could come from one of those top shelf jars: some harissa, pickled shallots or freshly made pesto all left from some recent use and waiting for another outing. An elevator could come from time taken with a technique like caramelising some onions. It could come from an unusual approach such as shaving on some beetroot or adding dried cranberries or roasted seeds. It might just be the look of something like a baby turnip which has caught my eye. These are all things that are in some way special. Don't be daunted by any recipe here because one element is not to your fancy or seems like too much trouble. These recipes are all about transfer, exchange and crossover. Look out for idea bases on the one hand and ideas for elevators on the other and then see what you want. Get these two right and your heart will be racing too.

AUBERGINE & RICOTTA
GRATIN

There are a handful of recipes that have been with me since I started giving cookery classes. This is one of them. My husband, Richard, and I were living in an apartment that had an open plan kitchen. Paddy Moloney of "The Chieftains" was our ridiculously generous landlord and instead of forbidding my business idea, he went out of his way to encourage it. The classes were demonstration only, with the punters in an arc around the counter. They wanted practical ideas that could be picked up after a single viewing, taking into account the distraction of a fair amount of chat and banter. This was the first recipe I taught to the first group (which included a few friends and neighbours to bulk up the numbers). It is adapted from the recipe given in Richard Olney's *"Simple French Cooking"*. The ricotta and Parmesan mixture that is poured over the top soufflées a little in the oven, creating a puffy, golden topping. It can stand on its own or accompany any number of dishes. I love it as much now as I did then.

Serves 6

TOMATO SAUCE
2 tbsp olive oil
1 medium onion, finely chopped
1 clove garlic, finely chopped
2 x 400g tin chopped tomatoes
½ tsp sugar
salt

3 large aubergines
olive oil, for cooking

RICOTTA TOPPING
110g ricotta cheese
1 egg
handful of freshly grated Parmesan,
   plus extra for the top
150ml cream
10 basil leaves

EQUIPMENT Ovenproof dish
   about 23cm x 20 cm

Preheat oven to 220°C, 200°C Fan, 425°F, Gas 7.

To make the tomato sauce
Heat the olive oil in a medium saucepan and add the chopped onion. Season with salt, cover with a lid and reduce the heat. Cook the onions for about 10 minutes until softened, stirring regularly. Add the garlic, cook out for a couple of minutes and then mix in the tinned tomatoes and sugar. Season. Simmer until the tomatoes have reduced to a thickish sauce, about 30-40 minutes.

To roast the aubergines
Slice the aubergine into rounds about 5mm thick. Pour some olive oil into a ramekin or small bowl and, with a pastry brush, paint both sides of the aubergine with the oil. Place the aubergine slices in a single layer on a baking tray (use a silicone mat if you have one). Season each slice. Roast in the oven for about 20 minutes, turning the aubergine slices over half way through the cooking. Cook until they are lightly coloured and totally tender. If they look a little dry when you turn them, paint the surface again with some olive oil and return to the oven.

To make the ricotta topping
Place the ricotta in a small bowl and break up with a fork. Beat in the egg and cream. Season and stir in a good fistful of Parmesan cheese and a few shredded basil leaves.

Assembling the gratin

Place a layer of overlapping aubergine slices in the bottom of the gratin dish. Spoon over a thin layer of tomato sauce. Scatter over some basil and a very light sprinkling of Parmesan cheese. Repeat, finishing with a layer of aubergine. You will not need all the tomato sauce for this recipe so keep any extra for another use. The gratin may be prepared up to this point in advance and refrigerated.

Just before placing in the oven, pour the ricotta mixture over the top and sprinkle with a dusting of Parmesan. Bake in the oven for about 25 minutes or until golden brown on the surface.

GRIDDLING AUBERGINES

My preference would be to griddle the aubergines for this dish rather than roasting them in the oven. To griddle aubergines, preheat the griddle until very hot and beginning to smoke. Slice the aubergines about 5mm thick. Paint one side with olive oil and place this oiled side down on the hot griddle. Leave the aubergines to cook until they become charred and lose their white fleshy colour. Paint the top side with olive oil, season with salt and then turn over and cook in the same way. If the aubergine slices still remain white between the griddle lines, then they are not yet tender and will require further cooking. At the end they should have a soft and yielding flesh. This is what makes them taste utterly delicious.

A variant of this gratin is the Italian dish Aubergine Parmigiana. The aubergines are griddled until fully tender (as above), then placed in overlapping layers in a gratin dish with tomato sauce. Each layer is topped with basil, a dusting of Parmesan and a few slices of mozzarella cheese. It is baked in the oven until the sauce is bubbling and the cheese melts and oozes into the tomato sauce.

GRATIN OF LEEKS
CHESTNUT MUSHROOMS
ROASTED CELERIAC & HAZELNUTS

This is a tasty, comforting and warming dish. Its two key ingredients are unfamiliar with the culinary limelight. A celeriac is used to sitting friendless and solitary among the other veg. Not many shoppers are drawn to celeriac's drab colour or knobbly skin. However, they are wonderful puréed, in a soup or here in a gratin. The wholegrain mustard, often used quietly in a dressing, also plays an important part here, lifting the sauce with its biting sweetness. Serve with some short grain brown rice or a tossed salad.

Serves 6

1 head celeriac
olive oil
salt
60g hazelnuts

2 fat leeks, white part only and
   3cm of the pale green
2 onions, finely sliced
1 bay leaf
3 small sprigs thyme, leaves
   pulled off the stem
3 cloves garlic, finely chopped

400g chestnut mushrooms, cut
   into quarters or eights,
   depending on size
30g Parmesan
12g butter
12g flour
150ml milk
1½ tbsp wholegrain mustard
freshly ground black pepper

70g sourdough or ciabatta
breadcrumbs
2 tbsp freshly grated Parmesan
2 tbsp olive oil
handful of chopped parsley

EQUIPMENT gratin dish about
   23cm x 20 cm

Preheat the oven to 220°C, 200°C Fan, 425°F, Gas 7.

To roast the celariac & hazelnuts
Cut a slice off the top and bottom of the celeriac and sit it flat on a chopping board. Using a serrated or chopping knife, remove the skin and any extra brown bits that lurk beneath. Chop into 1.5cm-2cm cubes. Line a tray with a silicone mat or baking parchment. Place the celeriac in a bowl, drizzle with the olive oil, season with salt and then scatter over the tray. Roast in the oven for about 20-25 minutes until it picks up a bit of colour on the edges and is tender on the inside. Turn the oven temperature down to 180°C, 160°C fan, 350°F, Gas 4. Place the hazelnuts on a tray and roast in the oven for about 5 minutes. Chop them into 2 or 3 pieces and set aside.

Cooking the leeks & onions
Split the leeks in half and fan the leaves under running water to remove any grit. Chop finely. Heat 2 tablespoons of olive oil in a saucepan and add the sliced onions. Season with salt, add the bay leaf and thyme and then turn the heat down to low. Cover and sweat slowly, stirring every so often, until the onions are translucent and tender. Add the chopped garlic towards the end of the cooking and, after a few minutes, add in the chopped leeks. Season and cook on a low heat, covered, for a further 10 minutes. The leeks should not pick up any colour. Place in a bowl with the celeriac.

To pan fry the mushrooms
Meanwhile, heat a frying pan and add a dash of olive oil. When hot, add the mushrooms, cooking them in two batches unless you have a very large pan. Toss over a high heat for a few minutes until they colour a little. After

a few minutes, season with salt and continue tossing for another minute until they are tender. Add to the leek mixture. Mix in half the grated Parmesan.

Making the white sauce

In a separate saucepan melt the butter, stir in the flour and cook over the heat for about 1 minute. Using a hand whisk, incorporate the milk little by little. Continue whisking and cook out for a few more minutes. Mix in the wholegrain mustard, the remaining Parmesan and season with salt. Combine the white sauce with the vegetable mix and add in two thirds of the toasted hazelnuts. Fold all the ingredients together and taste for seasoning. Place the mixture in a gratin dish. The mixture may be made in advance and refrigerated.

Parmesan crumb topping

Place the breadcrumbs in a bowl and drizzle in the olive oil. Rub the oil into the breadcrumbs and add the parsley, remaining hazelnuts and Parmesan. Sprinkle the topping over the vegetable mixture before baking. Cook the gratin at 180°C, 160°C Fan, 350°F, Gas 4 for about 25 minutes or until the breadcrumbs are golden. Serve immediately.

SHORT GRAIN BROWN RICE
CARAMELISED ONIONS, CAVOLO NERO
LEEKS & ROASTED SWEET POTATO

Some days I think this recipe is all about the rice. I always opt for short grain brown rice, even if it requires an excursion to the health food shop. This nutty, stubby grain is perhaps my favourite of any rice. The longer grain is just not the same. Sometimes I think the leeks are the unsung hero. You might not fully notice they are there, but it can be a mystery as to what keeps the rice so moist. On another day, it's the caramelised onions that grab my focus. Anyway, there is no need to prioritise which contributes most. It's not a contest. With these three ingredients, you have a base for a great vegetarian dish or an accompaniment to a pan-fried chicken breast.

Serves 4

2 sweet potatoes
olive oil
salt
400g short grain brown rice
3 leeks, white part only and 3cm
   of pale green
20g butter
3 onions, halved and sliced
   thinly crossways
200g cavolo nero, or other kale
Parmesan, freshly grated

Roasting the sweet potato
Preheat the oven to 180°C, 160°C Fan, 350°F, Gas 4.

Peel the sweet potato and cut into large bite-size chunks. Place on a roasting tray, drizzle with a little olive oil, season with salt and roast in the oven for about 20 minutes or until tender.

Cooking the short grain brown rice
Rinse the short grain brown rice. Put into a medium saucepan, add 1 teaspoon of salt and cover with 700ml of boiling water. Bring back to the boil, cover with a lid and turn down to the lowest setting. Cook gently for 35 minutes or until the water has evaporated and the rice is just tender.

Cooking the leeks
Split the leeks in half and fan under running water to remove any grit. Melt half the butter in a saucepan and mix in the leeks. Season, stir and cover with a lid. Sweat for about 10 minutes, stirring once or twice during the process. Do not allow the leeks to colour.

Caramelising the onions
Heat the remaining butter and 1 tablespoon of olive oil in a medium saucepan and add the onions. Season with salt, cover with a lid and cook on a gentle heat until the onions have softened, about 15-20 minutes. Stir occasionally during the process. Remove the lid and turn up the heat. Continue cooking until the juices of the onions begin to caramelise on the bottom of the saucepan. Scrape the bottom of the pot with a wooden spoon when it becomes golden so that the flavour will be absorbed back into the onions. Repeat the process, leaving the onions to

caramelise each time before scraping vigorously again. At the end, they will be golden all over.

Pull the kale from the stalks, rinse and chop roughly leaving it quite chunky. Add to the onions, stir and wilt down with the lid on for about 5 minutes.

When the rice is cooked, add in the leeks, caramelised onions, kale and the roasted sweet potato. Mix in a fistful of Parmesan and serve.

ALTERNATIVE VEGETABLES

The sweet potato can be replaced by other roasted vegetables such as peppers, aubergines, butternut squash, celeriac, white turnips or parsnips.

GNOCCHI
CHERRY TOMATOES
BUFFALO MOZZARELLA

It seems a shame not to have an Irish name for potato gnocchi – all those native ingredients and the Italians add a little Parmesan and run off with the credit. If I were passing a wonderful Italian delicatessen where they made their own gnocchi, I would give them a try but otherwise - you've guessed it - I would favour making my own. I would also oven-dry some tomatoes to heighten their intensity, both to use here and to have some for another day.

The sauce that is served with the gnocchi here is similar to a warm vinaigrette. The capers provide the acidity and the saltiness which balances the softness of the potatoes, the freshness of the semi dried tomatoes and the lusciousness of the buffalo mozzarella. Add a handful of rocket and you have a dish full of textures and flavours. It makes for a great starter.

Serves 4

300g cherry tomatoes
about 40 gnocchi, (see overleaf)
olive oil
2 cloves garlic, finely chopped
2 tbsp baby capers, (rinsed)
1 bunch rocket leaves
4 tbsp olive oil
1 packet buffalo mozzarella
10 basil leaves, chopped
freshly ground pepper
Parmesan, for grating

Preheat the oven to 100°C, 80°C Fan, 225°F, Gas ¼.

To make semi-sundried tomatoes
Cut each tomato in half and lay on a baking tray. Sprinkle with sea salt and drizzle over some olive oil. Bake for 1 hour or until the tomatoes are semi-dried. These tomatoes will hold in the fridge for a couple of weeks.

To pan fry the gnocchi
Heat 2 tablespoons of olive oil and add the gnocchi (you will probably have to fry them in two batches). Sauté until golden brown on both sides. Remove them from the pan.

Heat another tablespoon of olive oil in the pan and add the garlic. Cook gently without colouring for about 30 seconds before adding the capers and oven-dried tomatoes. Warm over the heat and then return the gnocchi to the pan. Toss the gnocchi and tomatoes together gently. Break the mozzarella into chunks with your hands and add to the pan along with the basil. Remove the pan from the hob. The mozzarella will soften slightly with the residual heat but will remain in chunks. Spoon the gnocchi onto plates and sprinkle with a generous dusting of Parmesan. Finish with a grinding of black pepper. Drizzle olive oil lightly over the rocket and scatter over the dish.

HOMEMADE GNOCCHI

The recipe for these wonderful gnocchi comes from Stephen Gibson of Pichet restaurant. They are quite sturdy and stand up to being panfried until golden which is part of their beauty. Lighter gnocchi, such as those often available in Italian shops, can just be blanched and added directly to the sauce.

Makes 40-50 gnocchi

800g Rooster potatoes to yield 500g
   cooked flesh
170g "00" flour (or strong flour)
80g Parmesan cheese, grated
10g salt
a fistful of flat-leafed
   parsley, chopped
a bunch of basil, chopped
1 whole egg
1 egg yolk

FREEZING GNOCCHI
Gnocchi are at their best freshly made, but they can be frozen. Dust a tray lightly with flour, place them in a single layer and freeze them immediately. As soon as they are firm, pop them into ziplock bags. They can be blanched directly from frozen.

Preheat the oven to 200°C, 180°C Fan, 400°F, Gas 6.

Prick each potato a few times with a fork. Place them on a baking tray, season with salt and bake in a preheated oven for about an hour until the potatoes are totally tender when pierced with the tip of a knife. Place the flour in a bowl with the Parmesan, 10g salt, chopped basil and parsley. As soon as the potatoes are cooked, cut each one in half and scoop out the insides. Press through a potato ricer (or use a potato masher). The potatoes should be warm when you rice them or otherwise the mix will be starchy. (The microwave is a great way to rewarm potatoes if necessary). Measure out 500g of potato and add all of the remaining ingredients, except for the egg and yolk. Mix all the ingredients together loosely with your hands. Beat the whole egg and yolk together. Pour into the potato mixture and gently bring the dough together.

While you are preparing the gnocchi, bring a large pot of water to the boil. Turn the gnocchi mix out onto a lightly floured surface. Knead gently, but briefly, until the potato mixture comes together. Cut the dough into 6 pieces and roll each piece into a sausage shape about 1.5cm deep. Cut with a knife or a dough scraper into pieces about 2.5cm in length. It is important to keep all the gnocchi the same size. Dust a tray lightly with flour and place the gnocchi on the tray.

Bring a large pot of water to the boil. Fill a large bowl with cold water and place beside the hob. Blanch the gnocchi in several batches by simmering them in the water for a few minutes. After 2-3 minutes, they will float to the surface. At this point they are cooked. Remove them with a slotted spoon to the cold water. Drain and then scatter onto a tea towel to absorb the excess moisture. Place in a container and drizzle with a little olive oil. The gnocchi may be prepared up to this point in advance, covered and refrigerated for a couple of days.

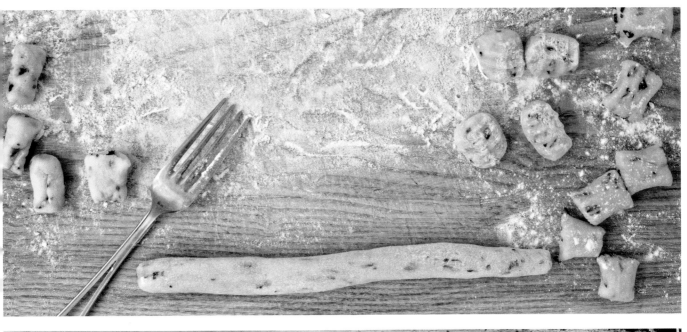

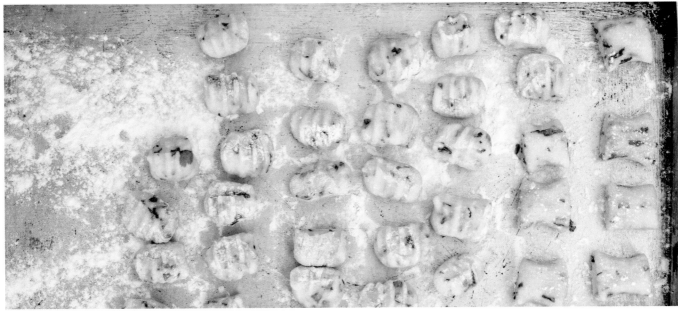

MOROCCAN FILO PIE
SPICED BUTTERNUT SQUASH, CHICKPEAS
HARISSA YOGHURT

This filo pie starts with the intrigue of the golden crispy pastry. As the knife breaks through the first slice, you get a glimpse of those colourful layers of squash, spinach and nuts. However, it is the taste that makes this a show-stopper. There is the hummus, the spices, the fruitiness. I like to have an accompanying yoghurt dip or some harissa but it really does not need much else. It's all in there already.

Serves 8

1 tsp ground cumin

1 tsp ground coriander

1 tsp paprika, plus extra for dusting

½ tsp ground cinnamon

½ tsp salt

olive oil, for panfrying

900g squash, peeled, deseeded and
   cut into small chunks

12 small round shallots, peeled
   and quartered (only 6 if they are
   the long banana shallots)

4cm root ginger, finely chopped

100g whole blanched almonds

100g shelled pistachios

75g dried cranberries

2 tbsp honey

225g fresh spinach

FOR THE HUMMUS

400g can chickpeas, drained
   and rinsed

2 cloves garlic, crushed

1 tsp ground cumin

2 tbsp olive oil

3 tbsp lemon juice

4 tbsp chopped fresh coriander

FOR THE FILO

100g butter

8 large sheets filo pastry

EQUIPMENT 28cm springform pan
   with removable base

Preheat the oven to 200°C, 180°C Fan, 400°F, Gas 6.

To make the filling
Mix the cumin, coriander, paprika and cinnamon, ½ tsp salt and 3 tablespoons of oil together. Put the squash into a bowl, pour over the spiced oil and mix with your hands. Scatter over a baking tray and roast in the oven for about 20 minutes or until tender.

Meanwhile, heat 2 tablespoons of oil in a frying pan and add the shallots. Season and cook, stirring regularly until they tenderise and start to colour. Stir in the ginger, almonds and pistachios. When the nuts turn a shade darker, add in the cranberries, honey and spinach. Toss until the spinach wilts. Remove from the heat and mix in the roasted squash. Set aside.

To make the hummus
Place the chickpeas in a food processor. Add the crushed garlic, ground cumin, 2 tablespoons of oil, lemon juice, two tablespoons of water and seasoning. Blend together. Taste and adjust as necessary. Stir in the chopped coriander.

To build the pie
Melt the butter in a small saucepan and brush the inside of the springform pan with butter. Brush one sheet of filo with butter and lay over half the tin so that it hangs over the edge by about 10cm. Brush a second sheet and lay it on the other side, allowing it to overlap the first sheet in the centre and to hang over the edge. Brush two more sheets of filo and lay in the opposite direction in the same manner. Build up two more layers in this way so that you use a total of eight sheets of filo. Pile half the squash mixture into the centre of the pastry. Spread over the hummus and then top with the rest of the squash mixture.

One at a time, bring the edge of each sheet of filo into the centre to cover the filling, creating folds as you go. Brush the surface with more butter. The filo pie may be prepared up to this point in advance and chilled.

To finish the pie
Bake the pie in the oven for about 30-35 minutes until the filo pastry is golden. Cut into slices and serve with the harissa yoghurt below.

HARISSA YOGHURT

300g Greek yoghurt
4 tbsp homemade harissa
  (see pg 43)
squeeze of lemon juice

To make the harissa yoghurt
Mix the harissa, yoghurt and lemon juice together and season with salt. Refrigerate until ready to use.

NO HARISSA? - NO PROBLEM.

No harissa in the fridge, then rustle up a yoghurt dip with cumin and mint. Mix together 300g Greek yoghurt, a bunch of finely chopped mint leaves, ¼ tsp ground cumin, ¼ tsp cayenne and ¼ tsp salt and serve with the pie.

TURKISH FLATBREAD

In many rural villages in Turkey, a communal oven is used for baking bread. Some time ago after engaging with a family at a local market, they invited me back to their mountain village. We made this yeasted yoghurt dough together, slid it into the clay oven and waited. I can't recall ever having enjoyed a bread as much. You may not have a clay oven out the back but eating these flatbreads hot off a pan or griddle is still a memorable experience.

Makes 10 flatbread

140ml warm water
1¼ tsp dried yeast
260g strong flour
1 level tsp salt
½ tbsp sugar
80g Greek yoghurt

To make the dough

Place 100ml warm water in a jug and sprinkle over the yeast. Stir and leave to prove for about 5 minutes. Combine the flour, salt and sugar in a mixing bowl. Stir the yoghurt into the water and yeast mixture and with one hand outstretched like a claw, gradually mix this into the flour. You will probably need to drizzle in a little more water, maybe 2-3 tablespoons until the dough comes together into a ball. The amount of water required will vary according to the type of flour you are using. The dough should be softish and only slightly sticky. If it is too sticky, add a little more flour. Remove from the bowl onto a lightly floured surface. Knead for about 5 minutes. Wash out the bowl, dry and then rub a drop of oil all over the inside. Place the dough back in the centre. Cover the bowl with clingfilm and set aside to rise for about two hours or until doubled in size.

Shaping the dough

Scoop the dough onto a lightly floured surface. Divide the dough into 10 pieces. Place the first piece of dough on an unfloured work surface. Working with unfloured hands, cup your right hand over the dough and using a little downward pressure, move in an anticlockwise direction until the dough forms a perfectly smooth ball. Place on a lightly floured tray. Repeat with the rest of the dough and leave to rest for about 15 minutes.

To bake the bread

Preheat a cast iron griddle or frying pan, or use a non-stick pan. Taking one ball of dough at a time, roll it out to about 2mm to 3mm thick on a lightly floured surface. Place directly onto the griddle or frying pan and cook for about 1 minute until brown speckles appear on the underside. Flip over onto the other side and repeat. Wrap in a teacloth or place in foil and keep warm in a low oven.

FLATBREAD, BEAN CHILLI
RED CABBAGE SALAD
GUACAMOLE & SOUR CREAM

A bean chilli can be used in all sorts of ways and has the advantage that it can be prepared long before it is needed. Don't be daunted by the long list of ingredients. This is really very straightforward to make.

I also want to persuade you to cook the flatbread. It requires a little yeast, a little rising time, a little shaping, a little kneading, a little rolling and then you have these flat doughs that you drop on to a hot griddle or pan. The slight char marks, the bubbles appearing on the surface as they cook, the incomparable smell and taste of a bread just off the pan invite relaxed eating together. It is not surprising that they are part of so many cultures across the world. You could buy ready made tortillas or Indian flatbreads but you would miss the thrill of making your own and of tearing the warm bread apart as it comes hot off the griddle.

Serves 6-8

2 tbsp olive oil
1 onion, finely chopped
1 bay leaf and a few sprigs thyme
1 stalk celery, finely diced
1 carrot, finely diced
4 cloves garlic, finely chopped
2 red peppers, finely diced
2 dried red chillies
2 tsp smoked paprika
2 tsp cumin
1 tsp oregano
½-1 tsp red chilli flakes (chipotle flakes, if possible)
2 x 400g tins chopped tomatoes
250ml vegetable stock, chicken stock or Marigold bouillon
1 x 400g tin black eyed beans
1 x 400g tin kidney beans
1 x 400g tin black beans

flatbreads (see previous page)
1 x 200g tub sour cream, to serve
pickled shallots or cucumber, optional (see pg 42)
guacamole, see overleaf
red cabbage salad, see overleaf

To make the chilli

Heat the oil in a medium to large pot and add the onion. Season with salt, stir, add the bay leaf and sweat slowly over a low heat, stirring regularly until the onion is tender, about 10 minutes. Pull the thyme leaves off the stalks and chop finely. Add the celery, carrot, garlic, thyme, peppers and whole dried chillies to the onion. Season and cook for a further 5-10 minutes. Add the paprika, cumin, oregano and chilli flakes. Cook for another few minutes before adding the tinned tomatoes and the stock. Simmer for about 15 minutes, with the lid off, until the tomatoes break down. Drain the tinned beans and add to the pot. Continue cooking until the sauce has reduced to a thickish consistency, about 30 minutes. Remove 2 large ladles of the bean stew, blitz in a food processor and mix back into the pot.

Meanwhile make the red cabbage salad and guacamole - see overleaf.

To serve

The flatbreads can be served hot from the griddle or frying pan but it is more practical to make them, wrap them in foil and keep them warm in the oven.

Serve the warm chilli in flatbreads with the red cabbage salad, guacamole, sour cream and pickled shallots or cucumber, if using.

RED CABBAGE SALAD

¼ small red cabbage, core removed,
  shredded finely
drizzle of olive oil
squeeze of lemon juice
salt

To make the red cabbage salad
Mix all the ingredients for the red cabbage salad together in a bowl and set aside.

GUACAMOLE

2 ripe avocados
1 spring onion, finely chopped
2 tbsp coriander leaves,
  finely chopped
1 clove garlic, finely grated on a
  microplane grater, or crushed
2 tbsp lime juice
salt
pinch chilli flakes, or chopped
  red chilli

Cut the avocados in half and remove the stone. With a large spoon, scoop out the avocado flesh and place in a mixing bowl. Using a fork mash roughly, still leaving some chunks. Add the chopped spring onion, coriander, garlic, lime juice, salt and chilli and mash a little more, leaving it with some texture. Taste and adjust the seasoning, adding more lime juice if necessary. Place clingfilm directly on the surface of the guacamole to prevent oxidisation. Refrigerate until ready to serve.

FLATBREAD
ROMESCO & BLACK BEANS

Barry Fitzgerald, the calm genius behind Bastible restaurant, gave me this recipe for his romesco sauce. I always add some chipotle chilli paste, an ingredient that is becoming more widely available. The romesco and chipotle mix is sometimes referred to as "chomesco" in our house, a name I am not reckoning will catch on. Chipotle chillies are used mainly in Mexican cooking and impart an earthy spiciness and a very distinctive smoky flavour. They are available in various forms but the ones that sneak their way into my pots are the chipotle chilli flakes and the chilli paste. Tread carefully with the paste, however, as it can be very hot and very smoky. Add it by cautious degrees.

It is the combination of flavours and textures with these flatbreads that is so appealing. If you don't have the time to make flatbreads, then griddle tortillas or heat them on a hot pan. The layers of "chomesco" with the crunch of the cabbage combined with the hearty black beans are very enticing. A great excuse to eat with your hands.

FOR THE BLACK BEANS
1 tbsp olive oil
1 large onion, finely chopped
2 cloves garlic, finely chopped
2½ tsp ground cumin
2 tsp smoked paprika
¼ - ½ tsp chipotle chilli flakes
   or regular chilli flakes
2 x 400g tins black beans, drained
   and rinsed
200ml chicken, vegetable stock or
   Marigold bouillon
good squeeze of lime juice
bunch of coriander, chopped

romesco, see overleaf

flatbreads (page 123) or tortillas

red cabbage salad, see
   previous page

OPTIONAL GARNISHES
150ml sour cream
pickled shallots or red onions
   (pg 42)
grated cheddar cheese or
   crumbled feta

Start by making the romesco (see overleaf).

To cook the black beans
Heat the oil in a medium sized pot and add the onion. Season with salt, cover with a lid and turn down the heat to low. Cook for about 10 minutes. Remove the lid and continue cooking for another 5 minutes until the onions begin to colour. Stir in the garlic, cook for 1 minute and then add the cumin, smoked paprika and chilli flakes. Cook out for a minute and then pour in the black beans and the stock. Season with salt. Simmer gently for about 5-10 minutes to allow the beans to pick up the flavour of the spices. Add the lime juice and the chopped coriander.

Place all the accompaniments in bowls on the table. Spread the romesco generously over the base of the flatbread, scatter over some red cabbage for crunch and top with the warm black beans. Serve with a spoonful of sour cream, some pickled shallots or cheese, if using.

ROMESCO

50g whole almonds
50g hazelnuts
6 plum tomatoes
1 red chilli
75ml olive oil
2 large cloves garlic, crushed
1 tbsp smoked paprika
2 tsp chipotle paste, or to taste
  OR 2 tsp tomato paste

Preheat the oven to 180°C, 160°C Fan, 350°F, Gas 4.

Place the almonds and hazelnuts on an ovenproof tray and roast in the oven for about 8 minutes. Turn the heat up to 240°C, 220°C Fan, 475°F, Gas 9.

Quarter the plum tomatoes and place on an ovenproof tray along with the chilli. Drizzle with a little of the olive oil. When the oven has reached the higher temperature, roast in the oven till tender and lightly charred, about 20-30 minutes.

When the nuts are cold, blitz in a food processor to fine crumbs. Remove to a bowl. Whizz the tomatoes, chilli, garlic, remaining oil, smoked paprika and chipotle paste to a purée. Remove and mix with the nuts. Season with salt. If you do not have any chipotle paste, you may add 1-2 teaspoons tomato purée to develop the intensity. After use, store in an airtight jar in the fridge. It will hold for about two weeks.

VERSATILE ROMESCO

Romesco is a rustic Catalan sauce which was traditionally made by the fishermen to go with seafood. It has many variants but typically contains almonds or hazelnuts, peppers or tomatoes, some chillies and often stale bread as a thickener. Try and choose really flavourful tomatoes and then make some final adjustments: maybe a little more vinegar for bite, some tomato purée for intensity or a little cayenne if not using the chipotle chillies.

Romesco can be served with lamb, pork or chicken, spread on bruschetta or used as a base for fish stew by adding white wine and broth.

CHICKPEA BURGERS
SWEET POTATO & PEAS

These vegetarian patties are very versatile. They were created by Noureia, my chief recipe tester for this book, who favoured the idea of adding some grated sweet potato and peas. If they are called burgers, they tend to get sandwiched into a bun with a selection on the table for everyone to build their own piles of tastes and textures: chutney, shredded vegetables, pickled shallots or whatever else comes from a raid on the fridge. Any leftovers the next day can become eastern patties and served with a spicy yoghurt dip (see page 270) or as part of an Indian meal. Change their name, change their character.

Makes 4 patties

1 medium sweet potato, about
   270g in weight
60g peas
200g cooked chickpeas
   (drained weight)
2 spring onions, finely chopped
1 green chilli, deseeded and
   finely chopped
2 cloves garlic, crushed (or grated
   on a microplane)
30g ginger, grated finely
3 tsp garam masala (page 248)
½ tsp turmeric
bunch of coriander, chopped
salt
squeeze of lime juice
gram (chickpea) flour, for dipping
   (or plain flour)
olive oil, for frying

4 burger buns
tomato or other chutney, for serving
red cabbage, carrot and apple salad,
   (optional), see overleaf
pickled shallots or cucumber,
   optional (pg 42)

Oven temp: 200°C, 180°C Fan, 400°F, Gas 6.

To make the chickpea burgers
Steam the sweet potatoes or cook in boiling water with their skins on. Check for tenderness by inserting the tip of a knife into the centre of the flesh. Allow to cool, then peel and grate coarsely. Blanch the peas in boiling water for 2 minutes. Drain and set aside.

Place the chickpeas, spring onions, green chilli, garlic, ginger, garam masala, turmeric and chopped coriander in a food processor. Season with salt, add a squeeze of lime juice and whizz until fine but still with a little texture. Taste and adjust the seasoning as necessary. Mix in the peas.

Divide the mixture into four and form into 4 patties with your hands. The mixture may be prepared ahead of time and refrigerated. If the mixture is a little wet, add 1-2 tablespoons of gram flour and mix in.

To cook the chickpea patties
Dip the patties in gram flour on both sides. Heat 2-3 tablespoons olive oil in a frying pan and add the chickpea patties. Cook for about 5 minutes on each side until golden on the surface and hot through. Alternatively, finish the patties in the oven at 180°C, 160°C Fan, 350°F, Gas 4. The patties may be panfried ahead of time, placed on a baking tray and then reheated in the oven closer to the time.

Char the burger buns on a griddle or heat under a grill. Spread chutney over one half of the bun. Sit the chickpea burger on top. Garnish with the red cabbage salad and pickles, if using. Top with the remaining half of the bun.

RED CABBAGE, CARROT AND APPLE SALAD

80g red cabbage, core removed
and finely shredded

80g carrot, grated

½ red apple, skin on

squeeze of lime juice

10 mint leaves, chopped

small handful coriander, chopped

1 tsp black or white
sesame seeds

1 tbsp olive oil

Slice the apple thinly. Stack the slices and chop into matchstick strips.

Combine all the ingredients in a bowl. Season and mix well. Serve with the chickpea burgers (see previous page).

COOKING CHICKPEAS FROM SCRATCH

If you wish to cook chickpeas from scratch, steep them overnight. As a rough guideline, you will get twice the volume of cooked chickpeas from dried i.e 1 cup dried chickpeas will produce 2 cups cooked. If you add bread soda to the soaking water (1 tsp for every litre of liquid), it will reduce the cooking time dramatically, from say 1½ hours to about 30-40 minutes. This is advisable particularly if the pulses have been sitting in the cupboard for a long time as their cooking time increases with age. Before cooking, pour away the soaking water, cover with fresh water and season with salt. It is a myth that adding salt to the water hardens the outer shell of pulses, preventing them from softening. Boil the chickpeas until tender.

ON AUBERGINES

The early flyers promoting the cookery school I ran from my home kitchen had a drawing of an aubergine on the front. Students who came for a season of my Tuesday evening classes used to say that there was no ingredient that would get me more excited. It wouldn't take much for me to launch into why I loved them, so here is my take on aubergines - scribbled thoughts and associations without recipe or measure.

My first urge with slices of aubergine is to paint them with olive oil. These can be thrown on a griddle or put in the oven on a roasting tray. The common mistake is not to cook them sufficiently. Don't be fooled by the early griddle marks or be tempted to take them out of the oven until they are really tender (see page 110 on griddling aubergines). Spoon some salsa verde, a tahini yoghurt or pomegranate molasses dressing over the slices, and you have a stunning base for a salad.

For shallow frying an aubergine, I like to use half olive oil and half sunflower oil. If the slices are salted generously for half an hour in advance (and then rinsed off and patted dry), this will draw out the moisture from the flesh and ensure that it will absorb much less oil. However, once the aubergine is cooked, I tend to opt for something saucy, often keeping in mind that tomatoes and garlic are an aubergine's other close friends. The aubergine and ricotta gratin in this book has been a favourite for as long as I can remember - layers of aubergine and tomato sauce, topped with a glorious ricotta, egg and cream mixture that puffs up in the oven.

Another option with the trusty griddle is to cook a whole aubergine to further heighten the smoky taste. Blast the heat and turn it every so often for half an hour until the outside becomes totally charred - yes, entirely black on the outside - and the interior is soft. This results in a warm smokiness that you don't get from oven baking. Scrape out the flesh from the inside and mix it with tahini, garlic, lemon juice, olive oil and mint or roasted cumin to make Baba Ghanoush. If I have friends over and am expecting it could be some while before we get down to eating, this is a dip to keep the energy going.

Aubergines work really well with anything from Indian spices to Thai salads. They are the most versatile vegetable. It is not just because you can halve them, slice them, dice them, purée them, shallow fry them or stew them, but because they complement so many other ingredients. Work your way around the favoured ingredients of each of the Mediterranean countries and you will see how well aubergines marry with so many vegetables, cheeses or spices. If I am shopping without an idea, then I will pick up an aubergine. It will make a meal out of just about anything.

MEDITERRANEAN TART
HARISSA ROASTED VEGETABLES

You can buy really good shortcrust pastry these days but always search for one made with butter. The time saved not making your own pastry can go into making the harissa that is such a vital feature of this tart. It is easily made and the result is not the blast of harsh heat that you often find in bought harissa. Instead the result is a heat with all sorts of spicy and smoky action in the background. It is spread here on the bottom of the tart and over the vegetables which are then roasted in the oven.

Serves 6

1 medium courgette
1 medium aubergine
2 red peppers
15-20 cherry tomatoes,
    halved
harissa (page 43)
2 tbsp olive oil
salt

shortcrust pastry, shop-bought
    or homemade (see page 141)
beaten egg, for brushing on the tart

FILLING
2 eggs
150g crème fraîche
200ml milk
salt and pepper
30g Parmesan

100g mature gruyère or cheddar

EQUIPMENT: quiche tin with
    removable base about 26cm wide
    and 3.5cm deep

Preheat the oven to 230°C, 210°C Fan, 440°F, Gas 8.

Chop the courgette and aubergine into bite-sized cubes. Core and deseed the red pepper and chop into similar sized pieces. Place all the chopped vegetables in a bowl, leaving aside the cherry tomatoes. Add 4 generous tablespoons of harissa and the olive oil and coat the vegetables. Pour them out onto a baking tray and roast in the oven for about 20-25 minutes until tender. Five minutes before the end, add in the cherry tomatoes.

Turn down the oven temperature to 220°C, 200°C Fan, 425°F, Gas 7.

Roll out the pastry and line the quiche tin. Place on an ovenproof tray and chill for 30 minutes in the fridge or 10 minutes in the freezer (my preferred method). Remove the tray and place a sheet of baking parchment inside the pastry case, making sure that it is large enough to come just higher than the sides. Fill the tart with ceramic baking beans or some dried pulses. Bake the pastry for about 15 minutes or until the edges of the pastry have turned a light golden colour. Remove from the oven, peel back the parchment paper and lift out the beans. Turn the oven down to 180°C, 160°C Fan, 350°F, Gas 4.

Using a pastry brush, paint the bottom of the tart with beaten egg (not the sides) and then return the tart to the oven for 5 minutes to crisp up the base. Leave the beans to cool and then return to the jar for another use. The tart shell may be baked to this point earlier in the day. Do not refrigerate.

Crack the eggs into a bowl and add all the other filling ingredients, except for the gruyère or cheddar. Beat lightly with a hand whisk or a fork just to break up the eggs.

Spread 3-4 tablespoons of harissa on the base of the prebaked tart shell. Scatter over the roasted vegetables and then sprinkle over the gruyère or cheddar. Pour the crème fraîche mixture over and around the vegetables. The filling should come to just below the rim of the tart. Bake in the oven for about 30 minutes or until the top is golden. At that point, press the tart very gently in the centre to ensure that the filling has set. If the top is getting too brown in the latter part of the cooking, turn the heat down slightly. When set, remove the tart from the oven and allow to cool a little before removing from the tin. Serve while still warm.

SOME USES FOR HARISSA

- Stir it into tagines or mix with chicken stock or Marigold bouillon to pour over couscous
- Blend with meat burgers
- Use it as a dip mixed with Greek yoghurt
- Spoon it over fried or poached eggs, or mix it into scrambled eggs
- Mix it into vegetables or potatoes before or after roasting.

BALSAMIC ONION TART
CHERRY TOMATOES
GOATS' CHEESE

The critical element of this stunning tart is the balsamic onions. Wedges of onion are covered with a combination of balsamic vinegar, sugar and thyme and roasted in the oven. It is tempting to eat them straight off the tray such is their intense sweet and sour flavour. I always roast more than I need so that, on another occasion, I can grab some from the fridge to put on bruschetta, to accompany cheese or to add to salads. Here, they are placed on the pastry as an extraordinary base for the goats' cheese and tomatoes.

Serves 6

320g shortcrust pastry, shop-bought
    or homemade (page 141)

BALSAMIC RED ONIONS
500g red onion
50ml balsamic
45ml olive oil
1 heaped tsp picked thyme
20g caster sugar
1 tsp salt

FILLING
2 eggs
6 leaves basil
150g crème fraîche
200ml milk
30g Parmesan
salt and pepper

80g St. Tola or another soft
    goats' cheese
16 cherry tomatoes, confit if you
    have them (see page 153)

EQUIPMENT quiche tin with
    removable base, 26cm wide
    and 3.5cm deep

Preheat the oven to 200°C, 180°C fan, 400°F, Gas 6.

To roast the balsamic onions
Slice the red onions through the root end into 2cm thick wedges. Mix the ingredients for the balsamic onions together in a bowl. Line a roasting tray with a silicone mat if you have one or cook the onions directly on the tray. Arrange in a single layer, keeping them fairly close together. Spoon the balsamic juices over the onions. Roast for 15 minutes, turn them over and roast again for about the same length of time. They should have a slight crunch at the end so don't overcook them. Set aside to cool. They will keep for a couple of months in the fridge.

To bake the pastry blind
Roll out the pastry and line the quiche tin. Place on an ovenproof tray and chill for 30 minutes in the fridge or 10 -15 minutes in the freezer (my preferred method). Remove the tray and place a sheet of baking parchment inside the pastry case, making sure that it is large enough to come just higher than the sides. Fill the tart with some dried pulses or ceramic baking beans. (Perhaps keep a jar of dried chickpeas strictly for this purpose). Bake the pastry for about 15-20 minutes or until the edges of the pastry have turned a light golden colour. Remove from the oven, peel back the parchment paper and lift out the beans. Using a pastry brush, paint the bottom of the tart (not the sides) with beaten egg and then return to the oven for 5 minutes to crisp up the base. Leave the beans to cool and then return to the jar for another use. The tart shell may be baked to this point earlier in the day. Do not refrigerate.

To prepare the tomatoes

If using confit cherry tomatoes, remove them from the oil. If using regular cherry tomatoes, make a little criss-cross through the skin on the base of the tomato. Have a bowl of cold water to hand. Place the tomatoes in a separate bowl and cover them with boiling water. Leave for 10-20 seconds until the skin loosens. Check one tomato before removing with a slotted spoon to the bowl of water. Peel off the skin and set the tomatoes aside.

To finish the tart

Crack the eggs into a bowl. Shred the basil and add to the egg. Mix in the crème fraîche, milk and about 20g Parmesan and season with salt and pepper. Beat lightly with a hand whisk or a fork just to break up the eggs.

Place a closely packed layer of balsamic onions in the bottom of the pre-baked tart shell, reserving some for the top. Crumble the goats' cheese over the onions. Pour over the egg custard, filling the tart to just below the rim. Arrange the remaining balsamic onions and the cherry tomatoes on top. Scatter the remaining Parmesan over the surface.

Reduce the oven temperature to 180°C, 160°C Fan, 350°F, Gas 4.

Place the tart in the oven and bake for about 30 minutes or until the top is golden. Shake the tart gently or press it gingerly in the centre to ensure that the filling has set. If the top is getting too brown in the latter part of the cooking, turn the heat down slightly. When set, remove the tart from the oven and allow it to cool a little before removing from the tin. It is at its best served warm but may be reheated.

SHORTCRUST PASTRY TART SHELL

There is an enormous satisfaction in making homemade pastry. After making it several times, you develop a feel for the consistency of the dough, so don't be put off if you don't get it right on the first attempt. Learning to roll out pastry is a very satisfying skill which becomes second nature the more you do it.

180g plain flour
90g cold butter, straight from
   the fridge
1 egg
drop of water, only if necessary

EQUIPMENT 26cm quiche tin
   with removable base

Making the pastry with a food processor

Place the flour and butter in the food processor and pulse until it resembles fine breadcrumbs. While the machine is running, add the beaten egg and whizz to blend without actually bringing the dough together. Open the lid of the food processor and check the consistency of the dough. Seal the lid and whizz again, adding a drop of water only if necessary (it depends on the size of the egg), and bring the dough together. Do not over process. It should be neither too firm nor too soft. Remove the dough to a lightly floured surface and knead for a few seconds just to bring the dough into a smooth ball. Wrap in clingfilm and press into a round disk, flattening the pastry with the heel of your hand. Allow to rest in the fridge for 45 minutes or in the freezer for about 15-20 minutes (be sure to set a timer). You are looking to chill the pastry quickly, not freeze it.

Making the pastry by hand

Alternatively, make the pastry by hand. Cut up the cold butter into very small cubes. Place the flour in a large bowl and add the butter. With a table knife in each hand, cut up the butter using a criss-cross motion, pulling the knives outwards like the radiating spokes of a wheel. Keep gathering the flour back into the centre and continue the cutting motion until the mixture resembles fine crumbs. Towards the end, using the tips of your fingers, rub the butter lightly into the flour. Bind with the beaten egg, adding a drop of water only if necessary.

Lining the tart tin

On a lightly floured work surface, roll out the pastry, allowing a little more than you think is required to cover the bottom and the sides. Always roll away from yourself and keep loosening the pastry by sliding a metal palate knife underneath. If the pastry is beginning to stick as you roll it, add another dusting of flour to the counter. If any cracks appear at the beginning, they can be pressed together. (If the pastry keeps cracking as you roll it, chances are that the dough is too dry and it requires another drop of egg or water). As you roll, dust the rolling pin every so often with a sprinkling of flour.

Roll the pastry to a uniform thickness between 3mm and 6mm. To lift the pastry into the tin, place the rolling pin about a third of the way from the top of the circle of pastry. With the help of a metal spatula, flip the top end of the pastry over the rolling pin so that it wraps around the pin. Lift up the rolling pin, holding the pastry in place with your thumb and first finger and unroll it loosely over the tin. Working very quickly, ease the sides of the pastry well down into the edges without stretching the dough. Trim the excess pastry so that it is level with the rim of the tart. Place the tart on a tray and refrigerate for 30 minutes or alternatively place in the freezer for 10 minutes. The pastry case may be lined in advance and refrigerated overnight. On occasion, I also bake the pastry blind the day before but in this case I do not refrigerate it.

Baking the pastry blind
Preheat the oven to 220°C, 200°C Fan, 425°F, Gas 7.

Place the quiche tin on a baking tray, line the pastry with baking parchment, fill with dried beans and bake for about 15 minutes. Check to make sure the paper will come away easily from the pastry. If not, leave in the oven for another 5 minutes. Remove the paper with the beans.

Reduce the temperature of the oven to 180°C, 160°C Fan, 350°F, Gas 4.

Using a pastry brush, paint the base of the tart with a little beaten egg and return to the oven for a further 5 minutes or so to dry out. Fill with the chosen filling and bake in the oven.

WILD RICE & BASMATI RICE SALAD
DILL, PECANS & DRIED APRICOTS

It is important with all the salads in this section not to get hung up on following the recipe to the letter. The trick is to be flexible, to develop the confidence to improvise. Wild rice is such a good start because it is unusually nutty and chewy, and can be combined with other less expensive varieties of rice. I have opted for some sweetness from dried cranberries and apricots but a rice salad can clearly go in any number of directions. Keep it interesting.

Serves 4

100g basmati white rice
1 tbsp olive oil
½ tsp salt
100g wild rice
75g pecans
40g dried apricots
30g dried cranberries

FOR THE DRESSING
1½ tbsp balsamic vinegar
2 tsp Dijon mustard
1 clove garlic, crushed
5 tbsp extra-virgin olive oil
1 small shallot, finely chopped
2 tbsp fresh orange juice
1 tbsp lemon juice
½ tsp salt

large bunch flat leaf parsley,
    chopped
small bunch of dill, chopped

Preheat the oven to 180°C, 160°C Fan, 350°F, Gas 4.

To cook the basmati & wild rice
Rinse the basmati in several changes of water. Drain through a sieve. Heat 1 tablespoon of olive oil in a small saucepan, add the rice and stir to coat with the oil. Mix in the salt and cover with 200ml of boiling water. Return to the boil, place a lid on the saucepan and turn the heat down to the very lowest setting. After about 12 minutes, check the rice. If it is tender and the water has evaporated, turn off the heat. Replace the lid and leave to sit for a further 5 minutes. Drain and spread the rice on to a tray to cool completely.

Bring a large pot of water to the boil and add the wild rice. Boil for about 25 minutes or until the grains are tender and some of the grains have burst open. They should have a chewy texture. Drain in a sieve. Spread out on a tray and leave until cold.

For the salad
Place the nuts on a tray and toast in a preheated oven for 5 minutes. Remove and chop into two or three pieces. Chop the apricots into slivers. Mix the apricots and dried cranberries in with the nuts.

Place the vinegar, Dijon mustard and garlic together in a small bowl. Gradually whisk in the oil until emulsified. Mix in the shallot, orange and lemon juice and season with salt. Set aside until just before serving.

Mix the basmati and wild rice in a serving bowl. Add the nuts, parsley, dill and dried fruit. Pour over about 6 tablespoons of the dressing and mix well. Taste and season with salt and pepper as required. Add more dressing if it needs it. Serve at room temperature.

RED QUINOA SALAD
BALSAMIC ONIONS, ROASTED SQUASH
FETA

If you ask people to name a "superfood", the one many propose is quinoa and some cite its use in the pre-Columbian civilisation in the Andes. The Incas did indeed revere quinoa but, to put it in perspective, it was ranked one down from the potato. The main reason that the UN dubbed quinoa a "supercrop" is because it is easy to grow and drought-resistant. My suspicion is that quinoa is the darling of the women's magazines because it is gluten free. I won't hold that against it. It makes a good backdrop here for one of my superfoods – balsamic onions. I use them elsewhere but this is where they started off in my cooking. I tend to use red onions as their sweetness works well. The secret is not to cook them past the point that they still have a very definite crunch. They are what makes this salad a "supersalad".

Serves 6

balsamic red onions, see overleaf

SALAD INGREDIENTS

1 small butternut squash or
   half a large one
olive oil
80g hazelnuts
2 tbsp pumpkin seeds
200g red quinoa

DRESSING

1 tabsp balsamic vinegar
½ shallot, finely diced
2 garlic cloves, crushed or
   grated on a microplane
45ml extra virgin olive oil
zest of 1 orange
zest of 1 lemon

bunch of basil leaves, chopped
bunch of flat leafed parsley,
   chopped
2 tbsp lemon juice, plus
   extra if required
70g feta
a handful of rocket leaves (optional)
sea salt

Preheat the oven to 200°C, 180°C fan, 400°F, Gas 6.

Peel the squash, remove the seeds and cut into rough 3cm cubes. Place in a bowl, season with salt and black pepper and drizzle with olive oil. Toss to coat and place on a roasting tray. Roast for about 25 minutes or until tender.

Place the hazelnuts and pumpkin seeds on a baking tray and roast in the oven for 5-8 minutes. Remove and set aside.

Add the quinoa to a pot of boiling water and cook on a steady boil for 10 minutes. Pour the contents of the pan into a sieve and allow to cool in the sieve.

For the dressing
Whisk all the ingredients together. Season with salt.

Combine all of the prepared ingredients in a bowl, holding back some of the balsamic onions for the top. Mix in the basil and flat leafed parsley. Dress the salad, season and add an extra squeeze of lemon juice if required. Crumble in the feta. Drizzle a little olive oil over the rocket leaves and add a pinch of sea salt. Fold into the salad. Spoon into a serving bowl and scatter over some extra balsamic onions.

BALSAMIC ONIONS

500g red onion
50ml balsamic vinegar
45ml olive oil
1 heaped tsp picked thyme
1 tabsp caster sugar
1 tsp salt

Slice the red onions through the root end into 2cm thick wedges. Mix the onions with all the other ingredients in a bowl. Line a roasting pan with a silicone mat if you have one, otherwise roast the onions directly on the tray. Arrange them in a single layer, keeping them fairly close together. Roast the onions for 15 minutes, turn them over and roast again for the same length of time. They should have a definite crunch to them at the end so don't overcook them. Set aside to cool.

BULGUR SALAD
CONFIT OF CHERRY TOMATOES
ROASTED VEGETABLES, PISTACHIO PESTO

This is a colourful salad thanks to the courgettes and peppers. However, the two ingredients that make it stand out are the bulgur and the tomatoes. Hunt down the really coarse bulgur, almost like pieces of short grain rice in size. The plump chewy grains add a texture to this salad which is different even from the medium grained version. The confit of cherry tomatoes comes from a renowned café in San Francisco called Gjelina. The tomatoes are cooked gently in olive oil, infused with slices of garlic, fresh basil and thyme. Keep a jar of them in your fridge, covered in their precious oil and you will find many uses for them.

Serves 8-10

confit of cherry tomatoes (page 153)

2 red peppers
olive oil
good quality balsamic vinegar

6 spring onions
2 small courgettes, sliced at an
    angle (1cm thick)
200g bulgur

PESTO
30g mint for the pesto, plus extra for
    the salad
30g basil for the pesto, plus an
    extra handful for the salad
30g pistachios
1 small clove garlic, crushed
80ml extra virgin olive oil
    or use the oil from the confit
    of tomatoes

1 tsp grated lemon zest, plus extra
    for the salad
salt

Start by making the confit of cherry tomatoes.

To roast the peppers
Preheat oven to 220°C, 200°C fan, 425°F, Gas 7.

Sit the red peppers on a tray and roast in the oven for about 25 minutes until the skin has charred slightly all over. Turn the peppers a couple of times during the process. Place on a chopping board and using the tip of a utility knife, remove the skin straight away. When the peppers are hot, the skin comes away easily. Remove the core and seeds from the centre and discard. Slice into thick strips. Plate, season with sea salt and drizzle with a little olive oil and balsamic vinegar. Leave to marinate.

To griddle the spring onion & courgette
Blanch the spring onions in boiling water for 30 seconds and refresh in a bowl of cold water. Drain and dry with kitchen paper. Preheat the griddle pan until just beginning to smoke. Brush each side of the spring onion with olive oil, season and place on the griddle. Cook on either side until slightly charred. Paint the courgette slices on each side with olive oil and place on the griddle. Season with salt. Cook for a couple of minutes on either side until charred but still crunchy. Remove immediately to a cold tray.

To cook the bulgur
Place the bulgur in a bowl and cover with boiling water. Seal with clingfilm and leave to sit for about 12-15 minutes. Taste the bulgur. It should be tender but still with a nice bite. Leave for a little longer if necessary. Drain, rinse in cold water and drain again.

To make the pesto

Strip the mint and basil off the stalks. Grind the pistachios in the food processor until fairly fine. Add the remaining ingredients except the oil and whizz briefly. Finally incorporate the oil. Do not overprocess. Place the pesto in a jam jar and cover with a layer of oil. It will hold in the fridge for several weeks.

Stir 4 tablespoons of pesto and the lemon zest into the bulgur. Chop some extra basil and mint and mix in, along with the courgette, roasted red pepper and spring onions. Taste and adjust if necessary. Finally, fold in half of the cherry tomatoes carefully. Spoon into a serving dish adding more cherry tomatoes on the top.

Place any of the remaining tomatoes/oil in a jar and keep refrigerated. They will hold for 2 weeks.

PAN FRYING COURGETTES INSTEAD OF GRIDDLING

Choose courgettes that are small to medium in size and are firm when pressed. Large courgettes can be quite bitter. If you do not have a griddle pan, the courgettes may be pan-fried at a brisk heat in a couple of tablespoons of olive oil. Cook in a single layer and season with salt while in the pan. Brief cooking is desirable so that they hold their texture in the salad.

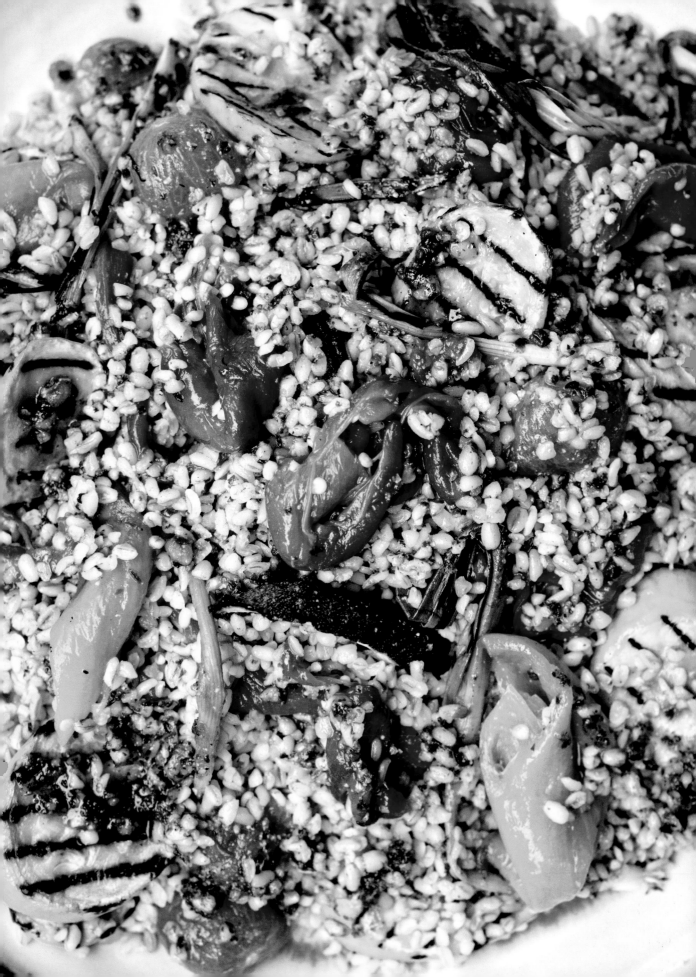

GJELINA'S
CONFIT OF CHERRY TOMATOES

Pop one of these into your mouth while they are still warm from the oven to see what the fuss is about. The soft, intense flavour explodes in your mouth – so familiar and yet so different. These tomatoes raise the bulgur salad to another level. They are delicious served over griddled fish, with all sorts of grains, or spooned over garlicky bruschetta along with some of their delicious oil. As they only last about 2 weeks in the fridge, eat them up quickly. Make sure to bring them back to room temperature before using. There is only enough in this recipe for the bulgur salad so if you want leftovers, make extra for that top shelf in the fridge.

350g cherry tomatoes
1 tsp sea salt
2 garlic cloves, smashed
6 basil leaves
2 fresh sprigs thyme
250ml extra virgin olive oil

Preheat the oven to 180°C, 160°C Fan, 350°F, Gas 4.

With the tip of a knife, make a little cross in the base of each tomato. Fill a bowl with ice cold water and place beside the hob. Add the tomatoes to a pot of boiling water for 15-20 seconds and then transfer to the water. Leave until cold. Gently slip the skins off the tomatoes and place them in an ovenproof dish where they will fit snugly in a single layer. Add the sea salt, garlic, basil, thyme and oil. Cover the dish with foil and bake in the oven for 30 minutes. The tomatoes should still hold their shape. Allow to cool and use, as required, in the salad. Any leftover tomatoes should be stored in a sterilised jar completely covered with the remaining oil. They will last for 2 weeks. The flavoured oil should also be put to good use. The tomatoes should be brought back to room temperature before using.

ROASTED POTIMARRON SQUASH
POMEGRANATE & MINT DRESSING
ST. TOLA GOATS' CHEESE

If I am serving a selection of salads, I would like at least one to be centred on a vegetable. I often turn to a butternut squash but its shyer cousin, the potimarron squash, is well worth seeking out. It stays firm in the oven, its skin is edible and it has the most striking colour. It is well suited to spices and here it is cut into crescents and roasted with a hint of cinnamon. The dressing is both a little sweet and a little sour which heightens the interest. What I love too is that this recipe is a good excuse to seek out St. Tola's goats' cheese. I stumbled across their farm in Co. Clare and spent a wet afternoon tasting all their cheeses. Amazing. If you are going to get lost in Co. Clare, can I suggest that Inagh is a very good starting point.

Serves 4

1 potimarron or large
  butternut squash
salt
3 tbsp olive oil
½ tsp cinnamon
½ tsp ground coriander

15g pumpkin seeds

POMEGRANATE MOLASSES &
MINT DRESSING
15g mint, finely chopped
½ pomegranate
75ml extra virgin olive oil
1 tbsp pomegranate molasses
  (or balsamic vinegar)
1 clove of garlic, crushed or grated
  on a microplane grater
zest of ½ lime
2 tsp maple syrup
1 tbsp lime juice

65g St Tola goats' cheese or
  another soft variety
½ tsp black sesame seeds

Preheat the oven to 240°C, 220°C Fan, 460°F, Gas 9.

To cook the squash

Leaving the skin on, slice the squash in half. Remove the seeds and any fibrous bits with a spoon. Cut into 3cm wedges and place in a bowl. Season with salt, sprinkle on the cinnamon and coriander and drizzle over the olive oil. Rub evenly over the squash and then place the wedges, cut side down, on an ovenproof tray. Bake in the oven for about 25-30 minutes or until the squash is totally tender and starting to colour. Remove and leave to cool. Turn the oven down to 200°C, 180°C Fan, 400°F, Gas 6. Scatter the pumpkin seeds on a baking tray and roast in the oven for about 5 minutes. Set aside until ready to use.

To make the dressing

Hold the half pomegranate in your hand with the cut side facing down over a wide bowl. Smack it with the back of a wooden spoon. The seeds and some of the pith will fall into the bowl through your fingers. Remove any bits of pith that have fallen into the bowl and discard.

Mix all of the ingredients for the dressing, except for the lime juice. Season and leave to sit for 30 minutes. This may be refrigerated for up to 2 days but bring it back to room temperature before serving and then mix in the lime juice.

Place the roasted squash on a platter, drizzle with the mint and pomegranate dressing. Crumble the goats' cheese on top and scatter over the pumpkin and sesame seeds. Sprinkle over some extra pomegranate seeds if you like.

FOOD PREFERENCES

If you scan through a cookery book, is your attention drawn to what you like or what you don't? And what happens when confronted with the unfamiliar? Most of us find that what is unknown tends to get lumped in with what we don't like. Our innate caution toward unfamiliar foods can easily turn to dislike. Some of us overcome our wary natures over time because life will have exposed us (perhaps through travel and friends) to many ingredients. But if exposure works so well, could we not overcome our aversion to any and every ingredient?

I had been pondering this question for some time when three elements came to my attention simultaneously: my then eight year old daughter, a bowl of olives and a persistent request for some much desired toy. An experiment suggested itself. The deal was that if she could eat a single olive every day for a month, then the toy was hers. The toy was obviously a mighty incentive because her facial register of disgust in the early days was quite alarming. By mid month, she was often voluntarily popping in a second olive and, by the thirtieth triumphant day, she had developed very clear olive preferences and had become something of a connoisseur. What was striking was not just that she came to love olives but how much her palate changed. She started to seek out gutsy and pungent flavours and became a demon for stinky cheese.

The New York food writer Jeffrey Steingarten took things even further. When he moved from practising law to writing about food, he decided that it would be unfair for him to review a restaurant given his haphazard range of food preferences and aversions. He set about eating every food that he did not like, a list that included anchovies, cranberries, falafel, refried beans and coffee ice cream. On average, it took about ten exposures for his distaste to disappear and he managed to purge himself of nearly all repulsions. As time went on, he found it increasingly difficult to make selections from a menu because all the choices seemed equally attractive. He reported that his only failure was desserts in Indian restaurants that, to his disappointment, remained "the taste and texture of either face cream or tennis balls".

So here's the challenge. Try not to skim over those recipes that wave an ingredient with an unfamiliar flag. When you find an occasional opportunity to be more daring, describe what you taste rather than dismiss it as disagreeable - otherwise liking food becomes synonymous with finding it familiar. And if everything has to be familiar, then you have constructed a flavour prison of your own making.

FISH

FISH

I worked for some months in a fish restaurant on the Italian Riviera. What can I say of my time there? Well, I can say hand on heart, it was the rudest, most sexist environment imaginable. I loved every moment. Underneath the male posturing of the chefs, there were some warm hearts and a real passion for cooking fish.

It might seem a challenge to work on a foreign coastline where almost all of the fish species were unfamiliar, but in fact this made little difference. After they are filleted, fish can usually be understood in terms of their thickness. In my mind, I would translate every fish to one I was familiar with ("this is a plaice, this is cod...") and away I would go. This is an important principle since availability depends so much on weather and season – it's better simply to enquire what is fresh.

The principles of fish cookery are the same the world over. It is sacrilege to overcook a piece of fish. The other habit to avoid is prodding and meddling with the fish while it cooks. There is generally just one quick flip and lots of careful watching. The more you cook fish, the more you become attuned to signs of it being ready. So in this busy Italian kitchen, it was the sounds and fast movement that were most striking - the fish hitting the pan, the oven opening and closing, the dishes plated up with speed ... and the constant shouting.

In this chapter I will set out the four ways in which I most commonly cook fish (with some suggested accompaniments). Then it's on to two of the marinades that are favourites in my fridge. I'll show you a few ideas for shellfish, a fish parcel, a tagine and a few takes on Asian ideas. All in all, they don't have too much in common with what they cook down on the Italian Riviera.

GENERAL POINTS ABOUT FISH

Fish should smell of the sea. If there is a 'fishy' smell, it means that the fish is past its best.

Fish must be refrigerated as soon as possible after purchasing. Ideally, remove the fish from its wrapping, place in a snug container and cover with a lid or some foil. Store in the coldest part of the fridge.

The flesh of fresh fish should be firm and bright. If the flesh looks tired or is an off-white colour (for white fish) - trust your instincts. It is past its best. If the flesh looks waterlogged, it has probably been sitting on ice, flesh side down, for too long or has been frozen. This will affect both the flavour and texture.

Eat fish as soon as possible after purchase and try not to hold it for longer than 24 hours as it deteriorates quickly.

Mussels should be covered loosely with a damp cloth or damp newspaper so that they can continue to breathe. They must never be sealed or covered with clingfilm. Wash in fresh water only before cooking.

Dry fish fillets with kitchen paper before cooking to ensure that there is no excess moisture on the surface.

Use a good quality non-stick pan for pan frying. If pan frying and roasting, choose a pan that is also ovenproof.

Make sure to have a good kitchen implement for turning the fish. My favourite is a small split-level metal palate knife. Some of the silicone turners are simply too thick and awkward to slide under delicate fish.

Heat the pan until beginning to smoke, then add the oil and place the fish in the hot pan. Don't move the fish at all or push it around at the beginning. This is what causes it to stick.

Heat control is essential. A high to medium/high heat is generally what works best when panfrying. Without sufficient heat, the water will start to come out of the fish and will prevent it from searing. With good heat control, the juices of the fish will caramelise on the bottom of the pan and give colour and flavour. The fish should then release easily from the pan.

PAN FRYING

This method is for thin fish like plaice or lemon sole which have already been skinned. It would also work for very thin fillets of John Dory, brill or turbot. The fish is dried thoroughly with kitchen paper and seasoned with salt. A non-stick pan is pre-heated to smoking point without any oil. The oil is then poured into the pan and when hot, the fish is added, presentation side down first. The secret is to keep the heat high so that the juices of the fish caramelise on the bottom of the pan. If the heat is too low, water will start releasing from the fish and it will stew, not sear. The fish is not moved until it becomes coloured on the underside. Then it is turned over onto the second side and cooked even more briefly. If a knob of butter is added for basting and flavour, then the heat is turned down a little. A squeeze of lemon juice is all that is required to finish.

SIMPLE PAN FRIED PLAICE
CHERRY TOMATOES & TARRAGON
BASIL MASH

If the fish is perfectly fresh, the simplest method is often best. One of the quickest accompaniments is to braise some ripe cherry tomatoes, throw in a single herb such as tarragon or basil and serve with basil mash on the side.

Serves 4

CHERRY TOMATOES
a knob of butter
1 shallot, finely chopped
1 clove of garlic, finely chopped
28-30 cherry tomatoes,
    sliced in half
2 tsp tarragon (or 12 leaves
    basil, chopped)
1 tbsp crème fraîche

4 fillets of plaice, skin removed
    (about 140g per portion)
olive oil
30-40g butter (optional)
good squeeze of lemon juice

Cherry tomatoes with tarragon

Heat a medium saucepan and add the butter. When melted, add the shallot and cook for a couple of minutes to soften. Add the garlic, stir for about 20 seconds and then put in the halved cherry tomatoes. Season with salt, turn down the heat to low and allow to cook with a lid for about 5 minutes or a little longer if they are not fully ripe. When the tomatoes begin to soften and release some of their juices, add in the chopped herbs and crème fraîche. Cook for another couple of minutes. Taste, check the seasoning and set aside until ready to use. The tomatoes may be prepared in advance and reheated.

To cook the fish

Dry the fish with kitchen paper and season with salt. Cook the fish in two batches or use two pans simultaneously. Heat a non-stick frying pan until smoking and add 1-2 tablespoons of oil. Place the fish in the pan, skinned side up and cook over a brisk heat until the underside has picked up some colour. Don't move the fish during this process and keep the heat fairly high. When the edges become tinged golden, peep at the underside to check

the colour. Turn the fish over and turn down the heat a little. Add the butter to the edge of the pan (if using) and when foaming, baste the fish. Cook the plaice for another 20-30 seconds on the second side. The timing will vary depending on the thickness but it will be mighty quick. Add a squeeze of lemon juice and slide onto warm plates along with any of the buttery, lemony juices.

BASIL MASH

Serves 4

675g potatoes
80g butter
150ml milk (or a combination of
  milk and cream)
bunch of basil leaves, finely chopped
salt

Peel the potatoes and steam until cooked. Mash or push them through a potato ricer back into the saucepan. Season with salt. Meanwhile, in a separate saucepan, heat the butter and milk and bring to boiling point. Add the hot liquid to the hot potato by degrees, beating with a wooden spoon to a smooth, creamy consistency. The exact amount of liquid required will vary with the type of potato. Check the seasoning. Just before serving, mix in the chopped basil. The mashed potato can be made in advance and zapped in the microwave in which case the basil should be added just before serving.

BEURRE NOISETTE

Beurre noisette with capers goes well with white fish. Pan fry the fish in olive oil as above and then remove to a warm plate. Give the pan a wipe out with kitchen paper and then add a generous piece of butter to the pan (20g per fish is good). Heat until the butter is foaming and goes light brown. Add some capers (about 1 teaspoon per person) to the pan and a squeeze of lemon juice and spoon the sizzling butter over the fish.

PAN FRYING WITH SKIN

This method is for fish such as sea bass, sea bream and mackerel. The aim here is to have crispy skin. Many of the same principles of the previous method apply here. The pan is heated without any oil. When the oil is added and hot, the fish is placed in the pan, skin side down. The fish can be pressed gently with a spatula in the initial phase of cooking so that it remains flat on the pan but then should be left undisturbed. The juices on the pan caramelise and crisp up the skin so that it releases easily. When the fish is turned over onto the second side, the heat is reduced. If the fish is very thin, the pan can be pulled off the stove and the second side can be left to cook briefly in the residual heat. The fish is removed immediately and served skin side up.

PAN FRIED SEA BREAM / SEA BASS
FENNEL & APPLE SALAD WITH HERBS

Most sea bream or sea bass are farmed and are much smaller than their wild cousins. These smaller fish allow for quick cooking and the crisp skin provides a textural contrast to the soft flesh of the fish. The fennel and apple salad is a perfect accompaniment to many types of fish: fresh and very tasty.

Serves 4

FENNEL & APPLE SALAD
1 fennel bulb
1 Granny Smith apple
2 stalks of celery
zest of half lemon
small handful basil
small handful flat leafed parsley
10-20 mint leaves, depending on size
1 stalk tarragon

FOR THE DRESSING
2 tbsp maple syrup
2 tbsp lemon juice
4 tbsp extra virgin olive oil
salt and pepper

4 fillets sea bream or sea bass,
   about 120-140g each, skin on
olive oil, for pan frying the fish

To prepare the fennel & apple salad
Chop the fennel stalks from the bulbs and discard, keeping any of the feathery fronds on the bulb (if there are any) for the salad. Cut the fennel in half through the root end and remove the core. Using a very sharp knife or mandolin, shave the fennel as finely as possible (this is important) and place in a bowl. Leaving the skin on, slice the apple thinly from top to bottom, turning the apple each time you come close to the core. Stack some of the slices and chop into julienne (thin matchstick pieces). Using a small utility knife, peel the fibres from the outside of the celery and slice thinly crossways. Chop the herbs. Put the apple, celery and herbs into the bowl, add the grated lemon zest and season.

Pour the maple syrup and lemon juice into a bowl. Whisk continuously while adding the oil. Season. Spoon the dressing over the fennel mixture (you may not need it all) and toss everything together.

To cook the sea bream or sea bass
Dry the fish with kitchen paper. Season both sides. Heat a non-stick frying pan and when hot, add 2 tablespoons of oil to the pan. When the oil is hot, place the fish in the

pan, skin side down. At the outset, press the fish gently in the centre with a fish slice to keep it flat, keeping the heat fairly high. After a few minutes, the skin will start to colour on the underside. When the edges of the fish become tinged golden, check the colour of the skin. If it is still quite pale, continue cooking at a high heat for another minute or so. With a fish this thin, ninety per cent of the cooking can be done on the skin side. Turn the fish over, remove the pan from the heat and allow the flesh to cook in the residual heat of the pan for the last 30 seconds. Place the fish on kitchen paper before transferring to a warm plate. Serve with the fennel and apple salad.

PREPARING FENNEL & APPLE IN ADVANCE

If you wish to prepare the fennel and apple in advance, fill a bowl with iced water. Squeeze in some lemon juice and add in the shaved fennel and apple. This will keep the fennel and apple crisp for up to an hour and stop them from discolouring. Be sure to dry them really well with a teacloth and then kitchen paper before coating with the dressing.

SEAR & ROAST

This method is for chunkier fish like cod, haddock, salmon, hake, halibut and thicker fillets of brill and turbot. This is combi-cooking, searing in the pan and then roasting in a high oven. Many of the same basic principles apply as in the earlier pan frying. The fish is dried and seasoned and placed in the pan skin side down (or on the side from which the skin has been removed). It is cooked at a medium heat for about five minutes. When the fish is turned over, it can be basted with a knob of butter. It is then transferred to the preheated oven for even cooking. The end result should still be moist and slightly rare in the middle.

ROASTED COD, SALSA VERDE
PURPLE SPROUTING BROCCOLI
WITH CHILLI & GARLIC
LEMON COUSCOUS

If the salsa verde is already in your fridge, then you are halfway there. It is such a tangy, colourful addition to lift a piece of cod. The crunchy broccoli is given the surprise of its life with the chilli.

Serves 4

LEMON COUSCOUS
40g pumpkin seeds, toasted
150g couscous
2 tbsp olive oil
120ml lemon juice
8 cherry tomatoes, chopped
4 large radishes, finely sliced
2 spring onions, finely chopped
bunch each of parsley, mint, dill and
  basil, chopped

BROCCOLI WITH GARLIC & CHILLI
500g purple sprouting or tender
  stem broccoli
olive oil
2 large cloves of garlic, finely sliced
a pinch of chilli flakes

4 x 150g cod, skin on
2 tbsp olive oil, for cooking
generous knob of butter (optional)

salsa verde, to serve (see overleaf)

Preheat the oven to 200°C, 180°C fan, 400°F, Gas 6.

To prepare the couscous
Place the pumpkin seeds on a baking tray. Toast them for about 5 minutes and remove. Put the couscous in a small bowl and drizzle over 1 tablespoon of olive oil, rubbing it into the grains with your fingers. Pour over the lemon juice (it should cover the couscous), seal with clingfilm and set aside for about 10 minutes to allow the grains to swell. Rub the couscous between your fingers to ensure that all the grains are loose. Mix in the rest of the ingredients along with the remaining tablespoon of olive oil. Season with salt.

To cook the broccoli
Trim off any coarse looking leaves or tough ends of stalk. Blanch the broccoli in boiling salted water for no more than 2 minutes. Refresh in a bowl of cold water. After a few minutes, drain and place on a tray lined with a teacloth. The broccoli may be blanched in advance. Warm 2 tablespoons of olive oil in a frying pan. Add the sliced garlic and chilli flakes. Heat gently until the garlic starts to pick up a little colour. Add the broccoli to the pan, season and toss with the chilli and garlic until well coated in the oil and heated through.

To cook the cod

Dry the cod with kitchen paper and season on both sides. Heat a non-stick pan until just beginning to smoke. Add the oil and place the cod in the pan, skin side down. Cook at a medium to high heat, allowing the skin to brown over a period of about 5 minutes. Don't move the fish around the pan. When the skin becomes golden, it will release naturally. Turn the fish over. Add a generous knob of butter to the pan (if using) and when it foams, tilt the pan slightly and baste the fish. Transfer to a preheated oven for about 5 minutes. The exact timing of the fish will vary slightly according to the thickness. What is important is that the fish remains really moist and slightly rare in the centre when it comes off the pan. The surface of the fish should be a milky white colour with the centre a little more translucent.

Slide the fish onto a warm plate and top with a spoonful of salsa verde. Serve the broccoli and couscous alongside.

SALSA VERDE

This vibrant salsa verde has a freshness from the herbs and a pungency from the capers and anchovies. Even if you think you don't like anchovies, they blend in here seamlessly and add a piquancy which enhances the flavour. Salsa verde is one of my 'elevators', one of those jars in the fridge which have so many uses. It will lift a piece of meat, potatoes or even a bruschetta but its impact on fish is perhaps the most stunning.

4 anchovy fillets in olive oil,
  drained
2 garlic cloves, crushed
large bunch of basil leaves
small bunch of chives, chopped
a fistful of flat-leaf parsley
  leaves
1 tbsp capers, drained
150ml extra virgin olive oil
1 tbsp lemon juice
salt

Put the anchovies, garlic, basil, chives, parsley and capers in the bowl of a food processor. Whizz until fine, intermittently scraping down the sides of the bowl. With the machine running, add in the oil and lemon juice. Do not overprocess. Remove and place in a bowl. Capers are very salty, so taste before seasoning further. The salsa verde will keep in the fridge for several weeks if stored in a jar with a film of olive oil poured over the surface. After each use, clean down the sides of the jar and top with another film of olive oil.

CAST IRON GRIDDLE PAN

A well-seasoned cast iron griddle is a great way to cook fillets of cod, salmon or hake. It imparts a smoky, barbecue-like note to the fish. A light pretender will not give the same result. There is a common fear that the fish will stick to a griddle but if you follow some basic techniques, it should release easily every time.

Developing a patina
After continued use, the griddle will develop a special coating, called a 'patina'. The patina is a result of the natural oils and fats from food baking onto the hot surface. This enhances the cooking performance of the griddle and means that foods will release easily. Do not use soap or heaving scouring pads to clean the griddle. A washing up sponge should be sufficient after soaking.

Principles of griddling fillets of fish
Buy fish with the skin on. The skin has natural oils and protects the flesh when it is turned over onto the second side.

Dry the fish with kitchen paper on both sides. Remove the pin bones with a fish tweezers. Season the fish with salt (and black pepper, if you wish).

Always oil the food, not the griddle.

Place the griddle over a strong heat. Preheat the pan for about 5 minutes before cooking. When it begins to smoke, turn down the heat just a little. You are now ready to start cooking.

Dipping in flour
There are two methods for cooking individual fillets on the griddle. The first and my preferred method, is to dip the flesh side (the non-skin side) in flour, shake off the excess and spread butter very lightly on this floured side as if buttering a slice of bread. The butter should be soft and at room temperature so that it spreads easily. The flour gives the fish a light crust. The fish is then placed on the griddle, buttered side down.

Brushing with olive oil
The second method, after patting the fish dry and seasoning, is to brush or rub olive oil over the flesh side just before cooking. The oiled side is then placed directly onto the hot griddle. Salmon is one of the easiest fish to cook this way as it has lots of natural oils and so the fish keeps basting itself. If you are hesitant about cooking fish on the griddle, it's a good one to start with.

When the fish hits the griddle, it should sizzle and smoke a little. If the smoke keeps billowing, then the heat was too high at the outset and should be turned down. Do not touch the fish. Keep cooking, without disturbing it, for a good few minutes until the edges start to colour. Then with a palate knife, have a peep at the underside. If it does not appear to have any colour, leave it a little longer. As it caramelises on the bottom, it should release easily when a thin spatula is slid underneath. When the flesh has well-charred griddle marks, turn over onto the skin side for the remainder of the cooking. The heat may need to be turned down a little at this stage. Remove the fish when it is still rare in the centre to ensure that the flesh is moist and delicate. If the skin does stick to the griddle pan, then simply slide the fish off its skin.

TOMATO & OLIVE SALSA

Once you have tried out any fish on the griddle, celebrate your achievement with this salsa.

Serves 4

1½ tbsp black olives, preferably
  Ligurian (or Kalamata),
  chopped roughly
1 tbsp capers, chopped
3 anchovies, preserved in oil
  (from a tin)
1 clove garlic, sliced thinly
  lengthways
85ml extra virgin olive oil
10 cherry tomatoes,
  chopped roughly
bunch of chopped basil

Place the olives, capers, anchovies and garlic in a saucepan with the olive oil and warm through gently. Be very careful not to overheat the oil. Remove from the heat, pour into a bowl and add in the chopped tomatoes and basil. Leave to infuse and to cool down.

The infused oil may be spooned over fillets of white fish such as cod, hake, plaice, turbot or sole and would also be lovely with chicken.

GRILLED MUSSELS
CORIANDER & COCONUT PESTO

Like many others, my first exposure to mussels was when they were covered with garlic butter, topped with breadcrumbs and placed under the grill. This is a more modern take with a coriander and almond pesto, topped with Parmesan cheese. I have yet to meet a single person who was hesitant about mussels who didn't become an instant convert when they tasted this combination.

Serves 4

32 large fresh mussels
generous dash of white wine
   or dash of water

FOR THE COCONUT &
CORIANDER PESTO
25g fresh coriander leaves
1 small garlic clove, crushed
2 tbsp ground almonds
2 tbsp coconut cream
2 tbsp olive oil
2 tbsp freshly grated Parmesan

To prepare the mussels
Knock off any barnacles that are attached to the mussels. Scrub the mussels thoroughly in several changes of cold water. Pull away any 'beards' which are attached to the shells. If any mussels are open, then press the top and bottom shell together. If they do not close tightly, then discard them. Any cracked mussels should also be rejected.

Put the mussels in a large saucepan with a generous dash of white wine or water. Cover the pan with a tight fitting lid and steam for about 4 minutes until the shells begin to open. The flesh is always at its plumpest as soon as the mussels open, so remove them one by one as this happens. With continued cooking, they shrink and become tougher. Discard any mussels which remain closed. When cool enough to handle, remove the top shell. The mussels may be cooked in advance, covered and refrigerated until ready to use.

To make the pesto
Put all the ingredients, except for the Parmesan, in a food processor and work into a rough paste. If you do not have a food processor, chop the coriander finely and add to the other ingredients. Spread some pesto over each mussel and sprinkle each one with a little Parmesan (the mussels may be prepared up to this point in advance). Sit the mussels on a baking tray. Place under a preheated grill until hot and the cheese is bubbling. Serve immediately.

NOTE Store the mussels in a container covered with damp kitchen paper or newspaper. Never cover with clingfilm. The mussels will keep for several days in the fridge. The mussels should smell fresh and briny, just like the ocean.

SEARED SCALLOPS
POTATO ROSTI
PEA PURÉE

Cooking scallops takes more courage than skill. The heat has to be sufficiently hot to sear in all those tasty juices and caramelise the surface. It needs decisiveness, too, to cook them ever so briefly on the second side. The pea purée is a perfect accompaniment and the potato rosti turns this into a spectacular main course. Of course you can do it.

Serves 4

PEA PURÉE
360g peas
1 tbsp cream
good pinch of sea salt
squeeze of lemon juice
100ml chicken stock or water
(or more if required)

POTATO ROSTI
3 large potatoes, preferably
Roosters or Maris Pipers
about 50g butter, clarified if possible
(see overleaf)

SCALLOPS
12-16 scallops
olive oil
squeeze lemon juice

EQUIPMENT: 4 ring cutters, about
7.5 - 8.5cm in diameter (the exact
size is not important)

To make the pea purée

Cook the peas in boiling salted water for about 2 minutes. Remove and place in a bowl of ice cold water. When the peas are cold, drain and whizz in a blender with the cream, stock and a good pinch of salt. Scrape down the sides of the blender with a spatula. Add a squeeze of lemon juice and blend again until totally smooth, adding more liquid if necessary. (If the pea purée is still too textured, pass it through a sieve). Taste and season as required. Set aside or refrigerate. There will be leftover purée at the end so keep this for another time.

To make the rosti

Peel and grate the potato on one of the biggest holes of the grater. Place the potato in a tea cloth, squeeze out all the excess moisture and then season with salt. Heat a thin layer of butter in a frying pan. Place the 4 cutters in the pan. Fill each cutter with potato to about 2.5cm thick and press down lightly. Cook the rosti on a medium to high heat until the underlayer of potato is completely golden and crispy. This will take about 5 minutes. Remove the cutters, flip the potato cakes and repeat on the other side until the potatoes are golden and tender throughout. The rosti may be prepared several hours in advance, placed on a baking tray in a hot oven (200°C, 180°C Fan, 400°F, Gas 6) and reheated close to serving.

To cook the scallops

Remove the little piece of muscle and coral on the side of the scallop and discard. Dry the scallops on kitchen paper. Just before cooking, season with salt. Heat a non-stick pan until beginning to smoke, add a good dash of olive oil and then place the scallops in the pan, being careful not to place them too close to one another. Cook at a brisk heat until caramelised on the underside which usually takes about 1 minute. It is important not to move

the scallops during this process. Turn them over, reduce the heat a little and cook for about another 30 seconds. Squeeze a drop of lemon juice over each one and remove from the pan. Serve with the potato rosti and and a swipe of pea purée.

BACON FOAM

For a final flourish, add a bacon foam. Bring 250ml chicken stock to the boil and add 150g smoked streaky bacon. Leave to simmer on a gentle heat for 10 minutes to allow the bacon to infuse into the stock, being careful not to allow it to reduce too much. Strain, reserving the liquid and discard the bacon. The foam can be made up to this point in advance. Reheat (but not to boiling), whisk in the butter and whizz with a hand blender to create a foam. Spoon over the scallops. This will be sufficient for about 8 people. It is not possible to make smaller quantities.

HOW TO MAKE CLARIFIED BUTTER

The milk solids in butter burn at quite a low temperature. Removing the milk solids decreases the risk of the butter burning and helps prevent the food from sticking. To clarify, melt some butter in a saucepan and bring it to the boil. When it bubbles once or twice, remove from the heat and allow it to rest for a few minutes. Strain the butter through a sieve, lined with a damp muslin. This will catch the milky solids and you will be left with clear butter. Alternatively, if you have no muslin, scrape the scum off the top and then very gently pour the clear butter into a small dish, leaving the milk solids behind. The milk solids may be discarded. Clarified butter will keep for weeks in the refrigerator but should be covered.

OLIVE OIL

I probably use olive oil nearly every day. If you don't get a thrill of excitement as you pick up a bottle, then it's probably because you have not had a great one, still in excellent condition.

Olive oil is something to relish. Be suspicious of cheap oil because, if it's the real deal, it is going to be expensive since harvesting relies so much on hand labour. It may sound extravagant but only buy extra virgin. Olives are pressed without the use of chemical solvents at temperatures less than 27°C (there is no "second pressing" as is sometimes suggested). If the oil meets a certain standard - the bar is not that high - it gets classified as extra virgin. If not, it is classified simply as "olive oil" or, a little misleadingly, "pure olive oil". This is substandard oil that is then refined, leaving it rather tasteless. The third category is "pomace oil" which is extracted from the waste of the olives (pulps, skins and pits) using chemical solvents. It should not be touched with a barge or any other type of pole.

Within the category of extra virgin, there is a vast range of taste and price. I like to have a less expensive, more mellow variety for cooking and then one more full-flavoured to pour over foods. The very best oils have labels that tell you not just where the oil came from but when it was harvested and bottled. These dates can be an important guide since olive oil does not improve over time. Unlike with most wine, olive oil is for immediate use. It's a good feeling to know that it does not need to be saved for a special occasion.

There are so many uses for olive oil. I like to use it to coat pasta or to make a salsa verde. It can be used as a marinade or to pour over some warm green beans, some roasted peppers, a grain salad. Olive oil has a particular affinity with tomatoes and bread, particularly if the latter is grilled. It is also great for cooking. I like to panfry fish or griddle my beloved aubergines in olive oil. There is a widespread myth that the smoke point of extra virgin olive oil is lower than other oils. It is not. No oil should reach the point when it starts to smoke but, contrary to what you read or hear, olive oil does not reach this point any quicker than other oils. It is worth pan frying slices of courgette or even frying an egg to see what a difference olive oil can make. When you have great ingredients, why would you ever want to start with a poor quality oil?

Olive oil is a luxury product that is good for heart and soul. It can turn the ordinary into the sublime. And so if I had a choice between a bottle of wine and a bottle of olive oil, I would definitely choose... both.

SAUTÉED PRAWNS
GARLIC BUTTER, CHERRY TOMATOES
CHARRED BRIOCHE

There can be a moment when a meal is taking a little time to arrive and hunger needs to be kept at bay. If you griddle some ciabatta, rub it with a cut garlic clove and drizzle on some olive oil, you have a base for anything to hand such as some ripe tomatoes with basil. This is a more considered version with the juice from garlicky prawns dripping on to griddled brioche. Very quick and very tasty. The leftover garlic butter can be stored in the freezer and used on steak or chicken.

Serves 4-6

FOR THE GARLIC & HERB BUTTER
100g butter, at room temperature
5 medium cloves garlic, crushed
15g parsley and coriander, leaves
   only (or use just one herb)
2 tbsp chopped chives
squeeze of lemon juice

FOR THE PRAWNS
24 tiger prawns, shelled
olive oil, for panfrying
salt
20 cherry tomatoes, halved
squeeze of lemon juice

4-6 slices brioche

To make the garlic & herb butter
Mix all the ingredients for the butter together. To make the butter in advance, wrap it in clingfilm, roll it into a log and twist the ends like a cracker. Wrap in tinfoil to ensure that the smell of garlic does not transfer to other food in the fridge.

To pan fry the prawns
To devein prawns, run a small utility knife along the back of the prawn and using the tip of the knife, remove the intestinal track if dark and visible. Dry the prawns with kitchen paper. Heat a non-stick frying pan and when hot, add about a tablespoon of oil. Add half the prawns to the pan, season and sear on a high heat. The prawns should colour a little before being turned and cooked on the second side for a further 30 seconds. Wipe out the pan with kitchen paper and repeat with the second batch. Now return all the prawns to the pan and add a couple of thick slices of garlic and herb butter. When the butter begins to foam, slide in the cherry tomatoes and turn down the heat. Cook for a few more minutes until the tomatoes soften. Finish with a squeeze of lemon juice.

Meanwhile toast the brioche on a griddle until charred lightly on both sides or place under the grill. Remove and drizzle with some extra virgin olive oil.

To serve, place a slice of brioche on each plate. Top with the prawns and tomatoes and all those garlicky, herby juices.

SALMON
SWEET SOY TAMARIND SAUCE
SAUTÉED PAK CHOI

On the top shelf of my fridge, I keep my sauces and marinades. They make for an easy meal after a tiring day. I got this wonderful recipe from Miriam Flores who used to come to the school to teach Mexican cookery. Having met a Cork man on her travels, she had been lured to Ireland. She created an extraordinary range of sauces and salsas which she sold at the Cork market before she and her husband returned to sunnier climes.

Her sweet soy and tamarind sauce can be made by hand. However, the result is infinitely better if made in a food processor. This breaks down the ginger and coriander seeds so the flavour of the sauce is more rounded. If you wish to make it by hand, grate the ginger before crushing it in a pestle and mortar along with the coriander seeds, red chilli flakes and garlic. The sauce benefits from sitting in the fridge even for a few days. The salmon dish below works well with the bean noodle salad (overleaf), or Thai or basmati rice.

Serves 4-6

SWEET SOY TAMARIND SAUCE
4 tbsp tamarind pulp (see page 249)
1 tbsp coriander seeds
50g ginger, chopped
4 cloves garlic, chopped
8 tbsp Thai sweet soy sauce
4 tbsp light soy sauce
1 tsp red chilli flakes
juice of 1 lime

2-3 pak choi
a drizzle of sunflower oil

4 x 160g salmon fillets, skin removed

bean noodle salad, optional
  (see overleaf)

To make the sweet soy tamarind sauce
Heat a saucepan or frying pan and add the coriander seeds. Shake the pan and toast the seeds for about 30 seconds. They will go a slight shade darker and will emit a toasted aroma. Remove and crush the seeds roughly in a pestle and mortar (or with a rolling pin). Place the ginger and garlic in a food processor and whizz until finely chopped. Add all the remaining ingredients and whizz again to blend. Pour into a jam jar and keep refrigerated until ready to use. It is best to use a sterilised jam jar if you wish to hold the sauce for several months in the fridge.

To cook the pak choi
Slice the pak choi in half lengthways and then each half into three wedges. In a frying pan wide enough to fit all of the pak choi in a single layer, heat 1 tablespoon of sunflower oil. When hot, add the wedges to the pan and sear for a few minutes before turning over onto the other side. Season lightly with salt and pour a couple of tablespoons of the sweet soy marinade into the pan. Cook until the pak choi is tender, adding a dash of water to the pan if the sauce is becoming too dry. Set aside while you cook the salmon.

To panfry the salmon

Dry the salmon with kitchen paper and season very lightly with salt. Choose a non-stick frying pan that is an appropriate size for the amount of fish and heat with a tablespoon of sunflower oil. Place the salmon in the pan, flesh side down first. Sear in the pan for a few minutes until golden on the underside. Turn the salmon over and pour over about 5 tablespoons of the sweet soy tamarind sauce. Baste it every so often but be careful not to allow the sauce to reduce too much or it may burn. If the sauce is drying out before the fish is ready, pour in a little water. The salmon should be served slightly rare. The exact timing will vary according to the thickness of the fish.

To serve, place the salmon on the plate. Spoon over some of the sweet soy tamarind sauce. Serve with the pak choi.

BEAN NOODLE SALAD

Vermicelli bean noodles, which are made from mung beans and water, are available in Asian markets. Spiked with a Thai dressing, lots of herbs and crunchy vegetables, they are a great Asian side dish. These noodles also work well in stir fries.

Serves 4

FOR THE DRESSING

2 red chillies, deseeded and
  finely chopped

a sliver of garlic, crushed

zest of 2 limes

4 tbsp lime juice

2 tbsp fish sauce

2 tbsp light soy sauce

4 tbsp palm sugar

FOR THE NOODLE SALAD

1 small carrot

½ cucumber

10 radishes

4 spring onions

180g vermicelli bean noodles

10 mint leaves, finely chopped

small bunch coriander,
  finely chopped

To make the dressing
Mix all the ingredients for the dressing in a small bowl.

To prepare the noodle salad
Chop the carrot into matchsticks. Split the cucumber in half, remove the seeds with a teaspoon and then slice thinly into half moons. Slice the radish as finely as possible. Remove the top 2cm from the spring onion and slice the remaining spring onion finely. Cut the noodles in half, pour boiling water over them and leave for 5 minutes. Drain and rinse with cold water. Mix the carrot, cucumber, radish, spring onion, mint and coriander into the noodles and pour over enough dressing to coat. The noodles are served cold.

KOREAN FISH PARCELS

Cooking fish in a parcel ensures that all the flavours are trapped inside as the fish steams. The fish sits on a selection of vegetables placed in the centre of the parcel and in this recipe a Korean dip is spooned over the top. If you have already made the Korean pancake in the brunch chapter, then you'll be laughing as the Korean dip will already be in your fridge. Banana leaves are available (fresh and frozen) in Asian markets and allow for a dramatic presentation though baking parchment is the best everyday option. The moment of opening the parcel is high drama for the senses.

Serves 4

FOR THE KOREAN MARINADE
100g Kikkoman soy sauce
20g sugar
1 tbsp gochugaru or 1 tsp
    chilli powder
40g shallot, diced very finely
2 spring onions, sliced finely
2 tsp sesame seeds
40g water

FOR THE PARCELS
120g courgette
half a small onion
4 spring onions
1 red pepper
60g carrot
1-2 green chillies
4 slices lime, cut in half
80g baby spinach

4 x 150g hake, cod, brill or
    turbot, skinned
¼ tsp black sesame seeds

Preheat oven to 220°C, 200°C Fan, 425°F, Gas 7.

To prepare the Korean marinade
Mix all the ingredients for the Korean marinade together and keep in a jar in the fridge. The marinade will hold refrigerated for a month.

To make the parcels
Halve the courgette lengthwise and then slice thinly crossways. Slice the onion as thinly as possible. Chop the spring onion into 1cm pieces. Slice the red pepper into thin strips. Slice the carrot into thin matchsticks. Chop the chillies into 3 or 4 pieces. Place all of the vegetables, including the lime, in a bowl and mix together. Season lightly with salt.

Fold a sheet of parchment paper in half and cut a semicircle approximately 18cm in radius. When the sheet is opened out, the circle will then be 36cm in diameter. Cut out four sheets and lay them all out on your counter top. Place the vegetable mixture on the lower half moon of each semicircle. Dry the fish with kitchen paper and season very lightly with salt. Sit the fish on top of the vegetables. Spoon about 2 tablespoons of Korean marinade over the fish in each parcel. To seal, fold over the free half of the paper so both ends meet and fold the edges in twice to seal them, creasing them carefully as you go.

Place the parcels on a baking tray. They should not overlap. Bake in the oven for about 10-15 minutes, depending on the thickness of the fish. Check one parcel in advance of when you think it is ready so that it doesn't overcook. Take into account that the fish will carry on cooking slightly after you remove it from the oven.

Serve immediately on hot plates. With a scissors, cut a slit down the centre of the parcel just as you go to serve it. You may eat the fish out of the paper to savour all the juices or tip the contents out onto the plate.

WRAPPING THE FISH IN A BANANA LEAF

For a dramatic Asian presentation, wrap the fish and accompanying ingredients in a banana leaf and close each one with wooden skewers or tie with cotton string.

If you wish to cook the fish parcels on the barbecue, soak the wooden skewers in advance. If the parcels are wrapped in two layers for the barbecue, the charred outer layer may be removed before serving, still leaving the inner banana leaf for presentation. It looks spectacular.

LAKSA
SALMON & PAK CHOI
BUTTERNUT SQUASH

The base of this dish is a wonderful curry paste that allows for much personal variation. As it develops, there is plenty of opportunity to add more heat but it is the use of the fish sauce that really allows you to determine how far to let off the breaks. This recipe cannot be followed exactly. Think of it as a guide. It requires you to taste as you go along and have the confidence to keep adjusting the fish sauce and chilli until your knees tremble.

Serves 4

LAKSA PASTE
4 lemongrass stalks
4 green chillies, seeds removed
2 cloves garlic, peeled
2 x 3 cm pieces of ginger, peeled
   and roughly chopped
zest of 1 lime
large handful coriander, leaves and
   stalks, roughly chopped

1 head pak choi
350g butternut squash, peeled
   and halved
100g dried rice vermicelli noodles
   (optional)
500g salmon, skin removed

2-3 tbsp sunflower oil
250ml chicken stock or
   Marigold bouillon
1 x 400ml tin coconut milk
2 tbsp fish sauce, or more
   as required

squeeze of lime juice
bird's eye chilli, chopped into
   thin strips, optional
handful of coriander,
   roughly chopped

To make the paste
Chop 1cm from the root end of the lemongrass and remove about 3cm from the top. Remove the outer layer and discard. Chop the remaining lemongrass roughly along with the chillies. Whizz all of the paste ingredients in a blender or mini food processor. It may need one or two tablespoons of water to get it properly blended. Scrape down the sides and blend again.

To prepare the laksa
Remove the leaves from the pak choi. Chop the leaves and the white stem roughly and set aside. Scoop out the seeds from the butternut squash and chop into large bite-sized cubes.

Soak the noodles (if using) in cold water till tender. Remove the bones from the salmon and chop into large bite-sized cubes.

Heat the oil in a wok. Add the spice paste and fry over a medium heat for a couple of minutes, stirring constantly. Do not allow the paste to colour. Pour in the stock and coconut milk and bring to the boil. Add 1 tablespoon of fish sauce, the butternut squash and simmer until tender, about 10-15 minutes. Taste and add more fish sauce by degrees to flavour the broth. The amount required will vary every time and the broth will also need fine-tuning at the end. Mix in the pak choi and the salmon. Simmer for 2-3 minutes. Drain the noodles and add them to the laksa. Stir to combine.

Just before serving, add a squeeze of lime juice and the chilli (if using). Scatter over the coriander.

SEA BASS
SPICED LENTIL BROTH & CORIANDER

This is an unusual dish with the spiciness of the lentils heightened by the fish sauce and served with a piece of poached or fried fish. I love brothy dishes, ones that I can almost slurp with a spoon. If the lentils absorb all of the liquid, just add some more stock or water to ensure that they stay swimming in their sauce. The crispy skin on the sea bass adds such an appealing contrast to the creamy lentils. It is the haunting flavour of the fish sauce which should linger at the end. I always serve this dish on its own in wide soup bowls.

Serves 4

2 tbsp sunflower oil
2 whole cardamom pods
1 star anise
3 shallots, finely chopped
4 cloves garlic, finely chopped
1 long red chilli, deseeded
    and finely chopped

160g cherry tomatoes (10-15
    depending on size), roughly
    chopped
¾ tsp turmeric
250g puy lentils
salt
1 litre chicken stock or
    Marigold bouillon

100ml cream
2 tbsp fish sauce, or more to taste
bunch of coriander

4 sea bass fillets, about
    120g - 140g each

For the spiced lentil broth

Heat the oil in a medium saucepan. When hot, add the cardamom pods and the star anise. After about 10 seconds, add the chopped shallots, garlic and chillies. Cook for a few minutes and mix in the cherry tomatoes, turmeric, lentils, salt and stock. Bring to the boil, lower the heat, and simmer for 20-25 minutes until the lentils are tender but still retain a slight bite. Stir in the cream and one tablespoon of fish sauce. Simmer for 5 minutes, taste and add more fish sauce as required. Remove the cardamom and star anise. The lentils may be prepared up to this point in advance.

Pan frying the sea bass

Remove the bones from the sea bass with a fish tweezers. Slice the fillets in half. Place the fish on the board, flesh side down and using a sharp knife, make little gashes in the central part of the skin about 2cm across. Dry the fish on kitchen paper and season both sides. Heat 2-3 tablespoons of oil in a large non-stick frying pan (cook the fish in two batches or in 2 pans if necessary). When hot, add the fish, skin side down. Using a fish slice, press the sea bass down gently in the centre to stop it from curling up. Keep cooking at a brisk heat, without moving the fish, until the skin turns golden. Most of the cooking will be done on the skin side so when you turn the fish, pull the pan off the heat and leave to cook for a further minute or two. Remove the fish and place on kitchen paper.

Meanwhile, reheat the lentils, adding a little more stock if needed to maintain a loose consistency. Chop the coriander, reserving some leaves for garnish. Sprinkle the chopped coriander into the broth.

Spoon into wide soup bowls and place the fish on top, skin side up. Scatter over a few coriander leaves to garnish.

ROAST BRILL
ASIAN TOMATO SAUCE
THAI RICE

This recipe has some key Thai elements. So much of Thai cooking is based on the balance of primary tastes - hot, sweet, sour and salty - and this complex tomato sauce has heat from the chilli, sweetness from the sugar, sourness from the vinegar and saltiness from the Thai fish sauce. The fun is in trying to get the balance right and when you are almost there, it is common for a drop of fish sauce to bring the whole thing together. I generally serve the fish with the sauce on its own but Thai rice and green beans with black mustard seeds (see page 279) would work really well here.

Serves 4

ASIAN TOMATO SAUCE
12 threads of saffron
3cm piece of root ginger,
 finely chopped
2 garlic cloves, finely chopped
1 large red chilli

2 tbsp sunflower oil
1 tsp black mustard seeds
300g tomato, peeled, deseeded and
 roughly chopped
2 tbsp white wine vinegar
150ml-200ml chicken, fish stock
 or Marigold bouillon
1 tbsp Thai fish sauce (nam pla)
1 tbsp palm sugar
pinch of chilli flakes (optional)
25g cold unsalted butter, diced
small bunch of coriander

4 brill fillets, about 150g each,
 skin removed
1-2 tbsp sunflower oil, for pan frying
 the fish
a knob of butter

To prepare the Asian tomato sauce

Soak the saffron in 4 tablespoons of boiling water. Peel and chop the ginger and garlic. Split the red chilli in half (remove the seeds if you wish) and chop roughly. Put the ginger, garlic and chilli in the bowl of a spice grinder or food processor and blend to a paste. If you do not have a grinder, grate the ginger, crush the garlic and chop the chilli finely and then pound to a paste in a pestle and mortar.

Heat a deep frying pan and add the sunflower oil. When hot, add in the mustard seeds. After a few seconds, the mustard seeds will start to jump and crackle. As soon as this happens, add the ginger garlic paste and cook for 2-3 minutes, stirring continuously. Add the diced tomatoes, white wine vinegar, stock, saffron and saffron water to the sauce. Simmer slowly until the tomatoes break down completely, about 8-10 minutes, adding more stock or water if necessary. Add the fish sauce and palm sugar and simmer for a few more minutes. Taste for balance and seasoning. If you would like a bit more kick to the sauce, add a pinch of chilli flakes. If it is too sweet, add another hint of vinegar. If its lacking depth, maybe it needs a hint more fish sauce. The sauce may be made up to this point in advance and then finished with the butter just before serving.

Whisk in the butter, one piece at a time and remove immediately from the heat. Ideally, the sauce should not be boiled when reheating.

To cook the fish

If the brill is thick, it may be started in the pan and finished in the oven. In this case, preheat the oven to 200°C, 180°C Fan, 400°F, Gas 6.

Pat the fish dry with kitchen paper. Season with salt on both sides. Heat a non-stick frying pan until very hot. Add 2 tablespoons of oil to the pan and when hot, add the fish flesh side down first. Cook undisturbed on a medium to high heat for 2-3 minutes. When the underside becomes a little golden, turn the fish over. Transfer the pan to the oven to cook for 3-4 minutes. Exact timing will depend on the thickness of the fish. Remove from the pan and place on kitchen paper.

Reheat the sauce, mix in the coriander leaves and serve with the fish.

THAI JASMINE RICE

Long grain Jasmine rice is the favourite rice in Thailand. Thai chefs who have come to the cookery school handle the rice almost reverentially. With cupped hands, they rub the grains together gently in several changes of water. The way they handle the rice is indicative of the important role it plays in their cooking. After witnessing this process, I am drawn to doing the same.

Serves 6

Thai Jasmine rice measured to the 425ml level in a glass measuring jug (400g rice)
1 tsp salt
700ml water

Start by rinsing the rice in several changes of water, very gently rubbing the grains together with your fingertips to remove the excess starch. Let the rice settle to the bottom of the bowl for a few seconds. Then tilt the bowl and pour off the water, holding the rice back with one hand if necessary. Repeat this process 4 or 5 times until the water runs clear.

Place the rinsed rice and salt in a medium pot and then cover with the water, traditionally about an index finger joint above the rice. Bring the water up to the boil, turn down the heat to its lowest setting, cover with a lid and then allow to cook undisturbed for 10-15 minutes. It is important not to stir during this time or the rice may become starchy. Towards the end of the cooking time, check the rice. If the grains on the top look a little dry, then sprinkle with a few tablespoons of water, return the lid and continue cooking on a low heat for a few more minutes. When ready, leave the rice to sit covered for at least a further 10 minutes before serving.

QUICK COUSCOUS

This quick couscous may be served with the tagine of hake overleaf. It will absorb all those lovely fish juices from the sauce.

Serves 6

450g couscous
1½ tbsp olive oil
475ml chicken stock, vegetable
   stock or Marigold boilllon
bunch of coriander, chopped

Place the couscous in a wide bowl and drizzle with the olive oil. Rub the oil through the grains with your hands so that they are lightly coated. In a saucepan, bring the stock to the boil and pour over the couscous. Mix quickly with a fork, cover with clingfilm and set aside for 10 minutes. Remove the clingfilm and use a fork to fluff up the couscous. Sprinkle over the chopped coriander. Serve warm.

TAGINE OF HAKE
FENNEL, OLIVES & RAISINS

When my friend Jane Beer texted me from Morocco about the extraordinary fish stew she had just eaten, I told her not to come home without the recipe. She did well. This is a one-pot dish which has a broth that catches so many Mediterranean flavours. It can be cooked in an unglazed Moroccan tagine if you are passing Tangiers or in a wide frying pan if not. All it needs is some couscous to mop up all those tasty juices. You may not be an olive lover but try the small Ligurian olives which blend perfectly here with the raisins, saffron and fennel to yield a broth that is light, fresh and has a natural fruity sweetness.

Serves 4

FOR THE TAGINE

12 threads saffron

6 tbsp olive oil

1 large onion, halved and sliced
    in rings

salt

3 heads fennel (or perhaps 2 if
    they are very large)

½ tsp ground ginger

50g raisins (giant raisins if possible)

60g black olives, preferably Ligurian
    or Kalamata (optional)

¼ tsp ground cinnamon, plus extra
    for the fish

¼ tsp ground cumin, plus extra for
    the fish

650g thick white fish, such as hake
    or cod, skin on

1 tbsp parsley, finely chopped

1 tbsp coriander, finely chopped

100ml water or vegetable stock

1 tbsp lemon juice

Place the saffron threads in a small bowl and cover with 2 tablespoons of boiling water.

Heat 2 tablespoons of olive oil in a wide, deep frying pan and add the sliced onions. Season with salt, stir and place a lid on the pot. Sweat the onions for about ten minutes until they begin to soften. Meanwhile, take the tops off the fennel and discard. Slice the fennel bulb in half lengthways and then cut into wedges about ½ cm -1cm wide. Add them to the pan and cook for about five minutes with the onions, stirring every so often. Add salt, ground ginger, raisins, olives (if using), the saffron and saffron water. Drizzle over 2 tablespoons of your best quality olive oil and continue cooking for about 3-4 minutes. Pour in about 100ml water, sprinkle over the cinnamon and cumin and cook for a further 10-15 minutes with the lid on or until the fennel is tender. (Check the tenderness with the point of a knife). The tagine may be made up to this point and set aside or refrigerated for later use.

To cook the fish

Remove the bones from the fish with a fish tweezers and slice into individual portions. Season with salt. Sprinkle each piece with a generous pinch of cinnamon and cumin and then top with the parsley and coriander. Check the amount of broth in the pot and add a little water or stock, if necessary. Bring up to simmering point and sit the fish on top of the fennel. Drizzle 2 tablespoons of extra virgin olive oil over the fish and add a squeeze of lemon juice. Replace the lid and steam until the fish is cooked but still moist in the centre. Serve immediately, perhaps with some couscous on the side.

ROASTED MONKFISH WITH CHIMICHURRI
JERUSALEM ARTICHOKES
BRAISED BABY POTATOES

Meaty monkfish can support big flavours so an Argentinian chimchurri sauce, which is generally served over grilled meat, works really well. It can be accompanied by all sorts of different vegetables but I urge you to try this suggested combination. Though it sounds sophisticated, the preparation is quite straightforward. The Jerusalem artichokes are quartered, drizzled with olive oil and roasted in the oven. You don't even have to go to the trouble of peeling the knobbly surface - just eat skins and all.

The braised baby potatoes are the final element, a favourite in our house since I tasted them in a little bistro in Paris. The potatoes are braised in stock with lots of herbs, some crushed garlic and a knob of butter until the liquid reduces to a coating glaze.

CHIMICHURRI
small bunch coriander, leaves only, chopped finely
small fistful parsley, leaves only, chopped finely
½ tbsp dried oregano
½ tsp smoked paprika
½ small shallot, finely diced
80ml extra virgin olive oil
salt and freshly ground black pepper
2 tsp red wine vinegar

JERUSALEM ARTICHOKES
400g Jerusalem artichokes
olive oil

ROASTED MONKFISH
1-2 tbsp olive oil
2 x 1.4 kg tails, bone in
1 sprig of rosemary
1 clove of garlic, bruised slightly with a knife
30g butter

braised baby potatoes, see overleaf
Jerusalem artichoke chips, optional (see note overleaf)

Preheat the oven to 200°C, 180C Fan, 400°F, Gas 6.

To make the chimichurri
Mix all the ingredients together, omitting the red wine vinegar. Refrigerate until ready to use but bring back to room temperature and stir in the vinegar before serving.

To roast the Jerusalem artichokes
Slice the Jerusalem artichokes in half or in quarters, depending on their size. Place on a roasting tray, season with salt and drizzle over some olive oil. Toss to distribute the oil and place in a preheated oven for about 25 minutes until golden brown and tender. These may be roasted about an hour or two in advance and then reheated in the oven.

To roast the monkfish
Even though monkfish tails are sold with the skin removed, there is generally a lot of trimming required. It is important to remove all the pinkish membrane with a small knife. Pat the monkfish dry with kitchen paper and season. Heat a frying pan and add the oil. Once hot, add the monkfish to the pan. Allow the fish to colour on the underside for 2-3 minutes and then turn over. Leave to brown on the second side for another minute or so before adding the butter, rosemary and garlic to the edge of the pan. Baste with the butter and then transfer the pan to a preheated oven. Cooking times will vary depending on the size of the monkfish - 8 minutes would be a good average. Remove and cover the pan with some tin foil. Allow to rest for 5 minutes. Remove the fish from the bone and

slice thickly. Plate and spoon over the chimichurri. Serve accompanied by the Jerusalem artichokes, the braised baby potatoes and Jerusalem artichoke chips if using.

BRAISED BABY POTATOES

600g waxy new potatoes, preferably smallish

500ml chicken stock or Marigold bouillon

salt

knob of butter for the cooking and also at the end

2 bay leaves

5 sprigs of thyme

1 sprig sage (optional)

3 cloves garlic, bruised slightly with a knife

Cut the potatoes in half (or into wedges if they are much larger) and drop them into a saucepan that will hold them neatly. Pour the stock over the potatoes, season with salt and add all the other ingredients. Simmer the potatoes until tender but still firm. Towards the end of the cooking, pour off most of the stock (keep for another use) and add another knob of butter. Reduce the liquid to a glaze which coats the potatoes. Check the seasoning and serve. If you wish to cook the potatoes in advance, whip them out of the liquid while still firmish (remember they will carry on cooking as they cool down) and lay out on a flat tray to cool. Finish as above.

SPECIAL GARNISHES

For a special garnish, try deep fried Jerusalem artichoke chips. Heat a saucepan of oil to 180°C, 350°F. Leaving the skin on, slice the artichokes as finely as possible (preferably on a mandolin), so they are almost transparent. Add the slices to the hot oil and cook for a few minutes until light golden. Remove with a slotted spoon, drain on kitchen paper and season with salt. These will stay crispy in an airtight container for about 3 days. They do not need to be reheated before serving.

Black radish, shaved thinly is another option as a quick garnish, as pictured overleaf.

MEAT

MEAT

One of my earliest food memories is of the last mouthful. I would hoard a small morsel of potato and veg and the last of my gravy so that I could relish, with closed eyes, the very last forkful of my roast chicken. I can still taste it. I still crave that last meaty mouthful. I hope that this chapter inspires different paths to that pleasure, whether it is with a simple roast duck breast or a long-simmered cheaper cut of beef and their varied accompaniments. Perhaps more than with any other ingredient, the route to great meat on the plate begins with what you buy. When I am going to have meat, I make a beeline for John O'Reilly's butcher shop in Mount Merrion. It's not an easy place to find. I have sent some people who never managed to find his premises and others who ventured up that mazy warren of streets and have never been heard of since. Nevertheless, it is important to have a good butcher. I have resisted the urge to preach about where you might find other ingredients but I feel strongly about this one. I am not referring to shops that buy in a whole pile of vac-packed meat and lay it out on trays. A real butcher knows the provenance of his meat. This is

Facing page: Braised beef short ribs - page 224

important, not only for my own health but for the influence I can bring to bear on how that animal lived and died - you can't sidestep the relationship between cheaper meat and unnecessary animal suffering. A butcher will also hang and age his meat. This takes time and space and causes the meat to shrink, none of which will appeal to a supermarket driven by profit alone. A butcher will also answer questions, in my case still patiently after twenty years. Go and find yourself one. It's a good investment.

PAN FRIED CHICKEN BREAST WITH THYME
PEPERONATA
ROAST BABY POTATOES

Simple as it may sound, there is a technique to cooking a humble chicken breast. What is ideal is to buy the chicken with the skin on, to season it well, and to start by cooking it at a medium heat in the pan until the skin becomes a rich golden colour. It can then be transferred to the oven with a few sprigs of thyme. The skin will continue to baste the meat, ensuring that it stays flavourful and succulent. The peperonata is a great side dish and this could be accompanied by some roasted baby potatoes with rosemary and garlic.

Serves 4

PEPERONATA

1 large onion

2 tbsp olive oil

1 clove garlic, crushed

1 tbsp sherry vinegar

2 red peppers, sliced into thin strips

2 green peppers, sliced into thin strips

1 x 400g tin chopped tomatoes

½ tsp sugar

salt

FOR THE POTATOES

800g baby potatoes

a few sprigs rosemary

olive oil

6 cloves garlic, unpeeled

FOR THE CHICKEN

4 chicken breasts, with skin on

salt and freshly ground black pepper

4-8 small sprigs thyme

olive oil, for cooking

a generous knob of butter

Preheat the oven to 200°C, 180°C Fan, 400°F, Gas 6.

To make the peperonata

Slice the onion in half and then crossways into thin rings. Heat the olive oil in a large heavy saucepan and when hot, add the onions. Season with salt, stir and turn down the heat to low. Cover and leave the onion to sweat until translucent and completely softened, about 10 minutes. Stir once or twice during the cooking. Add the garlic and cook for a further minute or two. Pour the sherry vinegar into the onions and boil for a few seconds before mixing in the peppers. Season with salt, cover the pot and cook at a medium heat for about 10 minutes. Pour the tin of tomatoes into the peppers and add the sugar. Bring up to the boil and then turn down to a simmer. Cook for about 10-15 minutes to allow the tomato mixture to concentrate in flavour and the peppers to soften. Check the seasoning at the end. The peperonata will hold in the fridge for up to a week.

To roast the potatoes

Slice the potatoes in half. Place on a roasting tray, drizzle with olive oil and season with sea salt. Mix the potatoes with your hands and then scatter over a few sprigs of rosemary and the garlic. Roast in the oven for about 40 minutes until tender.

To pan fry the chicken

Dry the chicken with some kitchen paper. Season both sides with salt and freshly ground black pepper. Heat 2 tablespoons of olive oil in an ovenproof pan and when hot, add the chicken, skin side down. Brown the chicken, without moving, over a medium high heat for about 8 minutes until the skin is a deep, rich golden brown. Place the sprigs of thyme sitting on the flesh as they cook. Tilt the pan and add a knob of butter to the front. When it sizzles, baste the chicken breasts. Turn the chicken over, leaving it to sit on the sprigs of thyme. Transfer to the oven and cook for a further 5 minutes or longer, depending on the thickness. In order to keep the chicken breasts moist, it is important to whip them out of the oven as soon as they are ready. Remove from the pan and leave them to rest on a warm plate for about 5 minutes, skin side up, so they retain their crispness. Slice and serve with the peperonata and roast potatoes.

A QUICK SAUCE

Spoon off any excess fat from the pan, deglaze the pan with a good splash of white wine, boil for a minute, add a little chicken stock (or Marigold bouillon) and reduce down. Finish with a knob of butter and some chopped herbs such as thyme, tarragon or oregano.

LAMB BURGERS
SWEET POTATO WEDGES
TZATZIKI

It is hard to beat a thick, juicy, homemade burger which is charred on the outside, tender and moist on the inside and accompanied by a variety of toppings. The cut of meat you buy will play a large part in the process and it is worth asking the butcher to mince it to get the result you want. Dipping roasted sweet potato wedges into a minty yoghurt sauce gives the satisfaction of getting stuck into a plateful of chips but without any deep fat frying, or guilt!

Serves 4

ROASTED POTATO WEDGES
600g sweet potato
2 tbsp olive oil
1 tbsp ground coriander

TZATZIKI
¼ cucumber
300g Greek yoghurt
1 small handful dill, finely chopped
a few sprigs mint, chopped
good squeeze of lemon juice

FOR THE LAMB BURGER
600g lamb mince, preferably
   from the lamb shoulder
2 tsp ground cumin
1½ tsp ground coriander
½ tsp paprika
½ tsp chilli flakes
1 clove of garlic, crushed
1 egg
olive oil, for cooking the burger

6 multi-seed burger buns

OPTIONAL GARNISHES
4 thick slices mature cheddar,
   or gruyère
a handful of salad leaves
pickled cucumber (see page 42)
caramelised onions (see overleaf)

Preheat an oven to 200°C, 180°C Fan, 400°F, Gas 6.

Roasted sweet potato wedges
Wash the sweet potatoes. Leaving the skin on, chop lengthways into wedges about 3cm thick. Toss them in a bowl with the olive oil, salt and ground coriander. Place on an oven tray, leaving enough space between each one so that they form a crust and brown. They will take about 25 minutes in the oven but should be turned after about 15 minutes.

Tzatziki
Peel the cucumber. Grate coarsely and place in a sieve over a bowl. Sprinkle with salt and leave for half an hour. Squash it with your hands and compress with a wooden spoon to extract the liquid. Mix the cucumber into the yoghurt. Add the herbs and lemon juice and season.

Lamb burger
Mix all the burger ingredients together in a bowl and season. Divide into 4 portions and shape the meat into patties. Heat a frying pan and add a dash of olive oil. When hot, place the burgers in the pan and cook at a medium high heat until they caramelise on the underside. Flip the burgers and brown the second side. Transfer to the oven for about 10 minutes, depending on the thickness. Add the slices of cheese for the final 4 minutes of cooking, if using.

To assemble the burger
Char the buns on a griddle or heat under a grill. Spoon some caramelised onions and pickled cucumber, if using, on one half of the bun. Sit the burger on top and finish with tzatziki, salad leaves and the other half of the bun. Serve with the potato wedges and extra tzatziki for dipping.

CARAMELISED ONIONS

2 tbsp olive oil

4 onions, cut in half and thinly sliced

1 sprig of thyme, leaves only

Caramelised onions

Heat the oil in a saucepan, add the onions, season and add the chopped thyme. Cover with a circle of parchment paper (called a 'cartouche') and then with a lid. Cook for 15 minutes on a low heat, stirring every so often. Then remove the lid, turn up the heat a little and cook for a further 15 minutes until the onions become lightly caramelised. As the juices of the onions start browning on the bottom of the pot, scrape the base vigorously with a wooden spoon. Scraping the pot regularly allows the caramelisation to be absorbed back into the onions. Continue this process until the onions are a rich golden colour.

CHICKEN SKEWERS
WITH POMEGRANATE MOLASSES
HARISSA ROASTED VEGETABLES
GIANT COUSCOUS

There is a riot of flavours going on here. The pearly couscous not only provides texture but is the perfect vehicle for absorbing those flavours. I am not fully sure why I find giant couscous so appealing but I suppose it's about size. The perfectly shaped beads are bigger than most grains and offer visual appeal as well as texture. Giant couscous is worth hunting down to experience what it can add to the harissa-coated vegetables and the juicy chicken skewers.

Serves 4
Makes 8 skewers

800g chicken breasts, without skin

CHICKEN MARINADE
3 tbsp pomegranate molasses
3 tbsp olive oil
1 tbsp honey
2 garlic cloves, crushed
1½ tsp Kashmiri chilli
  powder (see page 248), or
  ½ tsp regular chilli powder
1 tbsp cumin
½ tsp cinnamon
1 tbsp coriander
salt

GIANT COUSCOUS WITH
ROASTED VEGETABLES
1 red pepper
1 red onion
1 small aubergine
1 small courgette
12 cherry tomatoes, halved
4-5 tbsp harissa (page 43)
2 tbsp olive oil

250g giant couscous

olive oil, for cooking
flatbread, for serving (page 123)

Preheat oven to 220°C, 200°C Fan, 425°F, Gas 7.

To marinate the chicken
Chop the chicken into cubes about 2cm square. It is best to keep the chicken in pieces of similar size – thinner pieces may be folded in two on the skewer. Place all the marinade ingredients in a bowl and mix together. Add the chicken pieces and stir to coat. Cover and leave for several hours or overnight. If using wooden skewers, soak them in water for an hour or longer. After marinating, thread the chicken onto the skewers. Bring back to room temperature, ideally one hour in advance.

To roast the vegetables
Chop all the vegetables into bite size chunks. Add the cherry tomatoes to the bowl. Mix in 4-5 tablespoons harissa and 2 tablespoons olive oil. Season with salt and roast in the oven for about 20 minutes or until the vegetables are tender.

To prepare the couscous
Cook the couscous in boiling salted water for about 6 minutes. Drain well and spread out on a tray to cool. Mix with the roasted vegetables.

To cook the chicken
Turn the oven down to 200°C, 180°C Fan, 400°F, Gas 6. Season the chicken skewers. Heat a non-stick frying pan and add a dash of oil. Place the chicken in the pan and cook at a medium heat until golden (be careful as they burn easily). Turn over onto the other side and place in a preheated oven for about 8-10 minutes.

Serve the chicken skewers with the giant couscous salad and some flatbread.

PANFRIED DUCK BREASTS
RED ONION MARMALADE
POTATO GRATIN

Here is a special technique for rendering out the fat on duck breast which breaks with the norm for other meats. As the fat can burn quite easily, it is much better to start with a warm pan and slowly bring it up to temperature allowing the fat to render out gradually. With careful heat control, the whole layer of fat below the skin becomes deliciously, mouth-smackingly, crispy. Pair this with some red onion marmalade and potato gratin for a stunning combination.

Serves 4

RED ONION MARMALADE

2 tbsp olive oil

700g white onions, peeled and sliced

60g sugar

6 tabsp sherry vinegar

250ml full-bodied red wine

SAUCE

1 tbsp sherry vinegar

200ml meat stock or chicken stock

1 tsp Kikkoman soy sauce

4 duck breasts

salt and freshly ground black pepper

potato gratin, see overleaf

To make the red onion marmalade

Heat the olive oil in a heavy saucepan. Throw in the onions, season with salt, cover with a lid and turn down the heat to low. Cook very slowly for about 30 minutes, stirring regularly until the onions are completely tender. Remove the lid, add the sugar, vinegar and red wine. Cook for a further 20 minutes or longer until the liquid has reduced and has been absorbed by the onions. The end result should be neither too dry nor too liquid.

To make the sauce

To make the sauce, heat a dry saucepan until very hot. Add the sherry vinegar and boil for a few seconds. Add the stock and soy sauce and bring to the boil. Boil until reduced to about 150ml or until the sauce has concentrated in flavour. After cooking the duck, add in any meat juices.

To pan fry the duck breasts

Preheat oven to 180°C, 160°C Fan, 350°F, Gas 4.

Dry the duck breasts with kitchen paper. With a small sharp utility knife, score the skin and fat on each duck breast in a criss-cross pattern, keeping the lines quite close together. This will allow the fat to render out more easily. Season with salt and black pepper on both sides.

Heat an ovenproof pan until tepid and add the duck breasts, skin side down. Cook on a medium heat on the fat side for at least 5-10 minutes. The principle here is not only to ensure that the surface becomes a rich golden colour but that the underlying layer of fat renders out during the process. This cannot be done quickly so colouring the skin too fast will not achieve the desired result. During the cooking, pour the excess fat from the pan into a bowl (this may be kept for another use).

Intensely crisp skin is all about managing heat control and keeping the duck breast skin side down for the required length of time.

Turn the duck breasts over onto the flesh side and cook for a few more minutes. If the duck breasts are large, transfer the pan to a preheated oven to finish the cooking. Exact timing will depend on the thickness of the meat, how long it has been on the hob and how you would like it cooked. Remove from the pan and keep in a warm place, skin side up. Do not cover the fat or it will soften. Rest for 5 minutes before slicing and serving.

POTATO GRATIN

Many cooks hold strongly to their personal method for cooking a potato gratin. I have three preferences which I have stuck to over the years. I start with a combination of milk and cream so that the gratin is not too rich. Secondly, I am careful not to wash the potatoes once they have been sliced so that they retain their starch. Thirdly, I chop the garlic very finely and distribute it sparingly between the layers so that its flavouring remains subtle. The final result works well with every meat but it is the combination with red onion marmalade which reigns supreme.

Serves 4-6

250ml milk
200ml cream
butter, for greasing the gratin dish
1kg potatoes, such as Kerr Pinks
   or Roosters, peeled
salt
1 large or 2 small garlic cloves,
   finely chopped

EQUIPMENT Gratin dish about
   23cm x 20cm and 5 cm deep, or
   its equivalent

Preheat the oven to 200°C, 180°C Fan, 400°F, Gas 6.

Heat the milk and cream together to boiling point. Butter the gratin dish generously. Cut the potatoes into slices about 3mm thick. Place a layer of potatoes on the bottom, overlapping the slices slightly. Season with salt and scatter over some of the chopped garlic. Repeat the layering and seasoning, leaving the top layer free of garlic. Pour over the hot liquid so that it barely covers the potatoes and place in a preheated oven. After 15 minutes, press the potatoes down with a fish slice. You may do this once or twice during the early stages of cooking as the top layer of potatoes are inclined to curl up. However, never do this later on as you will break the skin which forms on the surface. The total cooking time will be about 1-1 ¼ hours. Reduce the oven temperature if the surface is becoming too brown in the latter part of the cooking.

The potato gratin can be made in advance and reheated in the oven. To reheat, drizzle a little cream (not milk) around the edges to keep it moist. This is not necessary if there is some liquid remaining at the bottom of the dish.

CHICKEN WITH SHERRY & DRIED PORCINI
BLACK PUDDING & CARAMELISED APPLES
ROASTED PARSNIPS & HONEY

There is something very homely about a casserole bubbling away in the oven, its flavours deepening and developing effortlessly. Braising meat on the bone, along with some aromatics, is generally the starting point. A further way to achieve real depth is to add some dried porcini mushrooms and some alcohol, such as the sherry suggested here. Black pudding, caramelised apples and parsnips take this dish in a distinctive and slightly less predictable direction but you may choose to vary these elements as you please.

Serves 4

15g dried porcini
150ml boiling water
2 tbsp olive oil
8 chicken thighs or a combination
   of legs and thighs, skin on, bone in
2 medium onions, thinly sliced
150ml medium dry sherry (such as
   Winter's Tale Amontillado)
200ml chicken stock or
   Marigold bouillon

a drizzle of oil, to cook the
   black pudding
200g black pudding, sliced into
   wedges about 1cm thick,
   skin removed
100ml cream

roasted parsnips, see overleaf
caramelised apples, see overleaf

Preheat the oven to 180°C, 160°C Fan, 350°F, Gas 4.

To prepare the chicken casserole
Place the dried porcini in a measuring jug and cover with 150ml boiling water. Leave to soak for about 15 minutes, then drain the mushrooms, keeping the valuable liquid. Discard any grit which may have fallen to the bottom of the jug. Chop the dried porcini finely and set aside.

Season the chicken on both sides. In a wide, deep, ovenproof frying pan, heat the olive oil and when hot, add the chicken pieces. Brown the chicken all over until the skin is a deep, rich golden colour, about 10 minutes. Remove from the pan and set aside. Drain the excess fat from the pan, leaving about 1½ tablespoons. Add the onions, season with salt and scrape up any crusty bits from the bottom. Place a lid on the pan and sweat the onions at a medium heat, stirring regularly until they become soft and translucent and pick up a little bit of colour, about 10 minutes. Stir in the dried porcini and cook for about 30 seconds. Deglaze the pan with the sherry, bring to the boil, then add in the stock. Return to the boil and then cover the pan, either with a lid or tinfoil. Place in a preheated oven for about 30-40 minutes or until the chicken is tender.

To cook the black pudding
Heat a non-stick frying pan. Add a drizzle of oil and place the slices of black pudding in the pan. Cook on each side for a couple of minutes. Add the black pudding to the casserole about 10 minutes before the end of the cooking.

At the end of the cooking, place the casserole on the hob. Add in the cream and boil for a few minutes, or longer if the sauce is still quite liquid. Taste for seasoning.

ROASTED PARSNIPS WITH HONEY

900g parsnips
2 tbsp olive oil
1 tbsp honey

CARAMELISED APPLES

2 Granny Smith apples
20g caster sugar
10g unsalted butter

For the parsnips

Peel the parsnips, cut in half and then into quarters or wedges. Place them in a roasting dish and season with salt. Drizzle over the olive oil and toss to coat. Place in the oven and roast for about 20-30 minutes until tender, turning them over half way through. Ten minutes before the end of the cooking, drizzle over the honey and return to the oven for the remainder of the cooking.

For the apples

Peel the apples, slice in half and then cut each half into thirds. Remove the core and discard. Pour the sugar into a heavy based saucepan and allow to caramelise until golden all over. Add the butter and swirl the pan. Place the apples in the pan and allow to caramelise on the surface, then turn them over and colour on the other side. Place a lid on the saucepan and cook at a gentle heat until the apples begin to soften.

THE WHOLE BIRD

You may use a combination of chicken breasts (skin on) for the casserole as well as legs and thighs. The chicken breasts will cook much faster so remove them after about 20 minutes (exact timing depends on the thickness) and then return them to the pan at the end of the cooking.

ON STOCK

My fervent hope is that, upon reading this, some reader who has never made their own stock might give it a try. If you feel that it's not worth the effort, I'll leave you well alone. Bear in mind that the time required is not really your time. The pot is just bubbling away quietly on the hob yielding up homely, comforting aromas.

The leftover carcass from a roast chicken is a good starting point for a stock. Any bones from the legs or thighs or any remaining succulent, crispy skin can be thrown in too. An alternative is to buy carcasses from a butcher. I still have a tall, trusty pot that was one of my first ever kitchen purchases that is ideal for this job. For a smaller batch, just buy a heap of chicken wings.

I worked with the incomparable Edinburgh chef Martin Wishart many years ago and he favoured making stock without the addition of any vegetable or even onion. I find this liberating as it means I don't have to fret if I am missing some of the ingredients I would usually like to throw into the pot. If they are to hand, I add any of the classic combinations of chopped onion, celery, carrot, a bay leaf, some peppercorns and a few sprigs of thyme; for an occasional Thai variation, I might try some chopped root ginger, bruised lemon grass and shallots, a few pandanus leaves knotted together, and some lime leaves. To make the stock, the bones should be barely submerged in cold water and then brought up to the boil. Skim any foam or impurities from the top and then turn the heat down to a gentle simmer. Bubbles should just be barely breaking the surface. (If it boils away madly, the stock will end up looking and tasting somewhat murky). Stock generally takes about 3 hours of gentle simmering at the end of which it can be strained and allowed to cool completely. For immediate use, allow the fat to settle and skim it off with a ladle. If you have the time, the stock can be refrigerated and the cap of solidified fat is then easily removed, leaving a bright, balanced flavour.

If kept in the fridge, the stock can be boiled up every three to four days and it will keep indefinitely. It is reassuring to have it sitting there, knowing a soup is just a few cooked vegetables away, a risotto not much longer. For a store of condensed flavour, briskly boil the degreased stock until it reduces to a fraction of its volume. Let it cool and pour into ice cube trays to be placed in the freezer overnight. The next morning, pour boiling water over the back of the ice cube trays and pop out the stock cubes. These are then a magnificent resource. When searing any fish or meat, the pan can be deglazed with some alcohol and these golden nuggets can be thrown in directly from the freezer with just a dash of water. They dissolve quickly. With just a few herbs or a knob of butter, there will be this glorious sauce. One taste of that and you will surely say that it was worth all that quiet bubbling.

BRAISED BEEF SHORT RIBS
HORSERADISH CRÈME FRAÎCHE
WILTED KALE, CANNELLINI BEANS

Any time I am unsure of a cut of meat, I race off to consult my butcher John O'Reilly. On one occasion, I remember clutching a cookbook so that I could show him the picture of American short ribs. "Jacob's Ladder" he said with barely a glance to the page. If your butcher looks at you quizzically, then just show him the photo! Braised for a number of hours until the meat is meltingly tender, this is the time to push the cutlery aside and gnaw on every last bit of succulent meat.

Serves 6

6 beef short ribs, about 2kg-2.7kg
salt
1 tbsp freshly cracked black pepper
1 tbsp thyme leaves plus 4
    extra sprigs
olive oil
2 onions, diced
2 carrots, diced
1 celery stalk, diced
3 bay leaves
2 tbsp sherry vinegar
200ml port
300ml full bodied red wine
500ml beef, veal or rich
    chicken stock

HORSERADISH CREAM
270g crème fraîche
2-2½ tbsp horseradish from a jar

WILTED KALE
2 cloves garlic, finely sliced
500g cavolo nero
2 tbsp olive oil

cannellini beans, see overleaf

Cut the short ribs into individual portions so that each piece includes a bone. Trim excess fat if necessary. Season generously with salt and pepper and sprinkle over 1 tablespoon of thyme. If time permits, refrigerate overnight or for several hours. Remove the ribs from the fridge an hour before cooking. Pat dry with kitchen paper.

Preheat the oven to 160°C, 140°C Fan, 300°F, Gas 2.

Heat 2 tablespoons of olive oil in a large sauté pan. Place the ribs in the pan in a single layer (you may need to cook the meat in batches) and sear until they are nicely browned on all all sides. This process will take about 15 minutes. Do not have the heat too high, otherwise the fat will burn. Remove the meat from the pan, set aside and drain off all excess fat. Add 1 tablespoon of olive oil to the pan and add the onions. Season with salt, stir to scrape up any crusty bits from the meat and allow to cook slowly with a lid on until the onions have softened, about 15 minutes. Mix in the chopped carrot, celery, bay leaves and thyme sprigs and continue cooking for another 5-10 minutes until the vegetables are beginning to caramelise.

Deglaze the pan with the sherry vinegar. Pour in the port and red wine and bring up to the boil. Reduce by about a third, add the stock and return to the boil. Pour the vegetables and stock into a suitable braising dish which will hold the meat in a single layer. Sit the meat on top of the vegetables, bone side up. The liquid should almost cover the ribs so if necessary, add a little extra stock. Cover the dish with foil and transfer to the oven. Cook for about 3-4 hours or until the meat is meltingly tender and comes away from the bone easily.

If not using straight away, allow to cool and refrigerate. The advantage of this is that the fat will solidify on the surface and can easily be scraped off with a spoon. If eating straight away, allow the juices to settle and skim any fat off the top. If the sauce is too light (this will depend largely on the stock that has been used), you may remove the ribs and reduce it down to concentrate the flavour. Return the ribs to the pot.

Horseradish cream

Combine the crème fraîche and horseradish in a small bowl. Taste and season. Jars of prepared horseradish vary enormously so adjust accordingly.

Wilted kale

Remove the green leaves from the kale and discard the stem. Wash thoroughly. Blanch the kale in boiling salted water for about 1 minute and refresh in cold water, then drain. Chop the leaves in half if they are too large. Heat the olive oil in a wide frying pan. When hot, add the slices of garlic. When the edges of the garlic start turning colour, add in the wilted kale. Season with salt and keep tossing the kale until heated through and tender.

Serve the short ribs along with some kale and cannellini beans. Spoon over some beef sauce and top with a blob of horseradish crème fraîche.

BEST EVER BEEF RIBS

To get the best, meatiest beef ribs imaginable, I suggest you track down a butcher who hangs his own meat, and ask him for the "Housekeepers Cut". This comes from the top rib and generally has 5 or 6 ribs joined together, which can easily be separated into individual rib portions or even divided in half lengthways to give smaller pieces. As this is a special cut, I need to request it at the beginning of the week before my butcher breaks down the carcass. This particular cut has a good layering of fat which helps to maintain its succulence but has a lot more meat on the bone than the short ribs. Well worth planning in advance!

BRAISED CANNELLINI BEANS

Braised beans are a hearty and comforting side dish to accompany the short ribs. They also work well alongside pork, chicken or even fish. The beans can be cooked without the lardons of bacon but perhaps replace them with a rind of Parmesan which will add a bit of soul.

Serves 6

250g dried cannellini beans, soaked
   in cold water overnight

1 tbsp olive oil

100g smoked bacon lardons

1 onion, finely diced

salt

1 small carrot, finely diced

1 stalk celery, finely diced

3 cloves garlic, crushed

1 x 400g tin cherry or
   chopped tomatoes

3 sprigs thyme

1 bay leaf

1.2 litre chicken, vegetable stock
   or Marigold bouillon

Heat 1 tablespoon olive oil in a medium saucepan and add the lardons. Sauté the bacon until the fat renders out and has picked up some colour. Add the onions, season with salt, cover with a lid and turn down the heat to low. Cook for about 10 minutes until the onions are tender and translucent. Add in the carrots, celery and garlic, cover and cook for a further 5 minutes. Drain and rinse the cannellini beans. Mix in the tinned tomatoes, thyme, bay leaf, cannellini beans and stock. Season with salt and bring up to the boil. Simmer for about 1½ hours until the beans are tender. After an hour, remove the lid and allow the liquid to reduce until it is the same level as the beans. The beans should be saucy at the end. The beans will hold for several days in the fridge.

GRATIN TOPPING FOR THE CANNELLINI BEANS

Mix 120g breadcrumbs with 3 tbsp olive oil, 3 tbsp freshly grated Parmesan, a handful of chopped parsley and 1 tsp chopped thyme. Pour the beans into an ovenproof dish, scatter over the breadcrumb topping and bake for about 30 minutes in the oven until the crumbs are golden all over.

SLOW COOKED PORK SHOULDER IN MILK
DRIED CHILLI, LEMON & SAGE
SWISS CHARD AND PARMESAN

When I worked in a family restaurant in Italy, I was asked to make this traditional north Italian pork dish which is cooked in milk. By the end of the cooking, I was a bit taken aback by the curdled sauce. The chef assured me that this was exactly how it was supposed to be. When you taste the whole dish, I guarantee that its appearance will not bother you either. Richard Gleeson, one of our memorably wonderful tutors now relocated to the wilds of Tipperary, used to make his own version, adding dried chilli, sage and lemon zest along with the herbs. Keeping these additions is a way of sending a warm salute in his direction.

Serves 6

1.8kg pork shoulder (weight on the bone) – ask your butcher to remove the bone and the rind
salt and freshly ground black pepper
2 tbsps olive oil
30g butter
6 cloves garlic, peeled but left whole
10 sage leaves
rind of ½ lemon, shaved into strips with a peeler
1 dried red chilli
325ml dry white wine
500ml whole milk

600g Swiss chard, washed and stemmed
20g Parmesan
zest of 1 lemon
squeeze of lemon juice
olive oil

crunchy roast potatoes (optional), see page 232

Slice the pork shoulder into 6 portions. Choose a deep-sided pot which will hold the 6 pieces of meat snugly. Season the meat with salt and black pepper. Heat a couple of tablespoons of olive oil in the pot and add the meat in a single layer (you may need to brown the meat in two batches). Sear the meat at a medium heat until golden on all sides and remove from the pot. Drain the excess oil and discard. Add the butter and when heated, throw in the whole cloves of garlic, sage leaves, lemon rind and dried chilli. Cook for a minute or so and then deglaze with the white wine. Return the pork pieces to the pot and bring the wine up to the boil. Turn the heat down to a simmer, cover with a lid and simmer on top of the stove, turning the meat a couple of times during the process. Top up the wine levels if necessary in the earlier part of the cooking. Ater 1½ hours, pour the milk into the pot and bring to the boil. The milk will probably curdle as you add it to the wine. This is perfectly normal so don't be concerned. After 3 hours of slow cooking, the meat should easily pull away from the bone with a fork and should be meltingly tender and succulent.

For the Swiss chard
Blanch the Swiss chard leaves for 1-2 minutes. Refresh in cold water, drain and pat dry. Chop the leaves roughly, leaving them fairly chunky. Dress the Swiss chard with lemon zest, salt, a squeeze of lemon juice, freshly grated Parmesan and a drizzle of olive oil.

Serve the pork and its sauce along with the Swiss chard. Crunchy roast potatoes are a great addition.

ROAST LOIN OF PORK WITH FENNEL & CORIANDER, CRACKLING CRUNCHY ROAST POTATOES

Many years ago, I took a trip to the River Café in London to write an article for the Irish Times. I was struck immediately by the sense of teamwork as they gathered to meet the morning vegetable delivery. I found myself partnered with a young trainee, one Jamie Oliver, podding peas and beans and brushing clean the huge variety of mushrooms with a pastry brush. Little did I know what would unfold for him! I had come from French kitchens with their bubbling vats of rich meat stocks. Here it was very different with chefs pounding herbs and spices with vast pestle and mortars. They relied on the residual juices from the meat and often just a dash of water or lemon juice to add to the roasting pan at the end of the cooking. This particular recipe is a characteristic way in which they would approach a loin of pork. The skin would be peeled off and crushed garlic, fennel seeds and coriander seeds would be spread liberally over the fat. The skin would then be tied back onto the pork so that there would be a layering of pork, garlicky spices and crackling. It's hard for my own taste buds not to go into overdrive just describing it!

To make your life easier, ask the butcher to remove the rind from the loin, leaving a thin layer of fat. The loin needs to be scored with a sharp knife with deep cuts about 5mm apart. I much prefer to do this task myself but it does take a bit of time. The scoring is essential to get good crackling.

Serves 6-8

10 garlic cloves, peeled
2 tbsp fennel seeds
2 tbsp coriander seeds
1 tbsp black peppercorns
3 tbsp sea salt
½ whole loin of pork with skin, rib end, about 2.75-3.25kg
juice of 2 lemons
3 tbsp olive oil

Preheat oven to 230°C, 210°C Fan, 450°F, Gas 8.

Pound the garlic, fennel seeds and coriander seeds together in a pestle and mortar. Add the black peppercorns and salt, then pound again. Rub the spice mix generously over the fat, into the cracks of the rind and over the meat. Replace the rind and tie securely with string.

Sit the loin on a rack on a roasting tray and place in the oven. Roast for about 20-25 minutes, allowing the rind to blister and brown. The high heat will get the crackling started. Turn the oven down to 200°C, 180°C Fan, 400°F, Gas 6 and pour over the lemon juice and 3 tablespoons of olive oil. Continue cooking the loin, basting it every so often for a further 30 minutes or so. The exact timing will vary so make sure to test the meat well in advance. If you have a thermometer, it will keep you from overcooking the pork. For the most accurate reading, place the thermometer into the thickest part of the meat, not touching the bone. You are aiming for a final temperature of between 63°C/145°F and 73°C/165°F. However, remember

that the internal temperature of the meat will continue to climb as it rests, so remove the meat at the lower temperature or even slightly less, say 60°C/140°F. Allow the pork to sit for about 15-30 minutes before carving.

CRUNCHY ROAST POTATOES

It is hard to beat roast potatoes cooked in duck or goose fat. They have the thickest, crunchiest exterior imaginable. On other occasions, I replace the duck fat with olive oil which also works well – delicious in their own way - but not as crusty.

potatoes, such as Roosters or
  Kerr Pinks
duck fat or goose fat
salt

Preheat the oven at 200°C, 180°C Fan, 400F, Gas 6.

Peel the potatoes, divide in half, if large, and cook in boiling salted water for about 8-10 minutes. Holding the lid over the pot, drain the potatoes well and then shake the saucepan vigorously a few times until the edges of the potatoes become fluffy.

Preheat a roasting tin in the oven for about 5 minutes with the duck or goose fat. Add the potatoes and season. Turn them in the fat so that the potatoes are coated and return to the oven. Alternatively, if you have a heavy cast-iron roasting dish that goes on the hob, heat a layer of duck or goose fat in the bottom of the dish. When hot, add the par-boiled potatoes, season and allow to colour lightly for a few minutes, then turn them over to get them coated in the fat. Transfer to the oven.

Continue cooking the potatoes for about 1 hour or until they are a rich golden colour all over. Turn the potatoes a few times during the cooking. You may turn the oven up to 220°C, 200°C Fan, 425°F, Gas 7 towards the end of the cooking if you wish to speed up the process.

Roast potatoes do not hold their crunchiness for very long after they have been removed from the oven so plan your timing accordingly.

ROAST CHICKEN
NAM JIM DRESSING

Nam jim is an extraordinary Thai dressing which is pounded together in a pestle and mortar in a matter of minutes. It is bold yet light and has a freshness from the coriander. The chicken is stuffed with bruised kaffir lime leaves and lemongrass stalks which have been pounded to release their flavour. The recipe here is for roasting the whole bird in the oven though for a quicker version, perhaps griddle some marinated chicken breasts (see the suggestion in the box overleaf) and serve with the same vibrant dressing. A great alternative is to cook the chicken butterflied or whole on the barbecue.

Serves 4-6

2 stalks lemongrass
4 kaffir lime leaves
1.2-1.5kg free range chicken
small bunch of coriander stalks
1 lemon, quartered
sea salt

NAM JIM DRESSING
2 garlic cloves, peeled
small bunch of coriander, roots,
    stems and leaves
sea salt
1 green bird's eye chilli*, chopped
1½ tbsp palm sugar
2 tbsp fish sauce
3-4 tbsp lime juice
1 small shallot, or 2 Thai shallots,
    finely chopped

* if possible purchase the small green chillis available in the Asian market that measure about 5cm in length

Preheat the oven to 200°C, 180°C Fan, 400°F, Gas 6.

To roast the chicken
Bruise the lemongrass all over with a pestle or bash with a rolling pin. Bruise the kaffir lime leaves in your hand and push the lemongrass and lime leaves into the cavity of the chicken, along with a bunch of coriander stalks and the quartered lemon. Rub a little olive oil over the skin of the chicken and season with sea salt. Place the chicken in a roasting tin slightly bigger than the chicken itself and bake in the oven for about 1-1 ½ hours depending on the size of the chicken.

If you have a thermometer, test to see if the chicken is ready by inserting it into a meaty part of the leg (avoiding the bone). You are looking for a final temperature of 73°C/165°F but remember that the meat will climb a few degrees as it rests so it is best to remove the chicken at about 70°C/160°F. Allow the chicken to rest for about 10-15 minutes before carving.

While the chicken is cooking, make the nam jim dressing.

Nam Jim dressing
Put garlic, salt, coriander roots (if you have them) and a few chopped stems into a pestle and mortar and pound until they begin to form a paste. Add the chilli and pound again. Mix in palm sugar, fish sauce and lime juice, then stir in the chopped shallots. Taste and balance the dressing by adding more lime juice, fish sauce or palm sugar as required. The nam jim should be sweet and sour, hot and salty.

Slice the chicken and spoon over the nam jim dressing.

GRIDDLED LEMON CHICKEN BREASTS

Marinate 4-6 chicken breasts, skin side up, in 4 tablespoons of olive oil, 4 tablespoons of lemon juice, 2 bruised cloves of garlic and some seasoning. Leave for several hours but ideally overnight. Remove from the marinade, pat dry and griddle or barbecue until tender. Slice and spoon over the nam jim dressing.

GRIDDLED OR BARBECUED BABY AUBERGINE

Preheat the griddle (or barbecue) for 5 minutes. Slice the aubergines into halves or quarters and season with salt. Brush some olive oil over the flesh using a pastry brush. Place flesh side down on the hot griddle and cook, undisturbed, for a few minutes. Repeat for each side until fully cooked, brushing with more olive oil as needed. They should be completely tender when pierced with a knife. The aubergines go really with the Nam Jim.

HOMELY ROAST CHICKEN & STUFFING
POTATO BOULANGÈRE

It's a pity that cooking a whole chicken seems to have gone out of fashion. I never tire of cooking a whole bird on the bone, the herby buttery stuffing inside and all those caramelised bits stuck to the bottom of the roasting tin ready to make a light sauce. For the potato boulangère, meltingly sweet onions nestle between layers of sliced potatoes and cooking them in stock leaves them flavourful, light and moist. Hopefully at the end, there will be some leftovers for the next day and a chicken carcass to throw into the pot to make stock.

HERB STUFFING
45g butter
1 onion, finely chopped
150g white bread, such as ciabatta
large bunch of parsley, chopped
bunch of basil, chopped
a few sprigs thyme, picked and
　finely chopped

1.2-1.5kg free range chicken
2 tbsp olive oil, plus extra to rub
　on the skin
sea salt
bunch of basil or oregano, chopped,
　for under the skin

FOR THE SAUCE
100ml white wine
200ml chicken stock or Marigold
　bouillon
squeeze of lemon juice

EQUIPMENT: Ovenproof dish
　about 23cm x 20cm

potato boulangère, see overleaf

Preheat the oven to 200°C, 180°C fan, 400°F, Gas 6

To make the stuffing
Heat the butter, add the onion and season with salt. Turn down the heat to low, cover with a lid and cook until the onions are tender. Meanwhile whizz the breadcrumbs in a blender or food processor. Remove to a bowl, add the chopped herbs and onion and mix together. Allow the stuffing to cool if not cooking the chicken straight away.

To roast the chicken
Place the chicken on a chopping board, chop off the wing tips and reserve them for the stockpot. Catch the skin at the tip of the chicken breasts and gradually separate it from the breast meat on either side of the breast bone. Be careful not to tear it. You are aiming to create two large pockets with your fingers the full length of the breast meat. Tip the chicken on its end and sprinkle some sea salt into the pockets. Push the chopped herbs under the skin and try to spread them all over the flesh on each side as best you can. Draw the skin back to cover the meat. Push the stuffing into the cavity.

Place the chicken in a roasting tin slightly larger than the chicken. Rub olive oil all over the skin and then sprinkle generously with sea salt. Place in a preheated oven and cook for about 1-1½ hours, depending on the size of the chicken.

To make the sauce
When the chicken is tender, remove it from the oven and allow to rest for about 10-15 minutes before carving. Remove the chicken from the roasting pan. Tilt the pan so that the juices pool in one corner. Remove any excess fat with a spoon. Place the roasting pan on the hob and deglaze the pan with the white wine, scraping up any

crusty bits from the bottom of the pan. Boil the juices for about a minute and then add the stock. Boil for a further couple of minutes, add a squeeze of lemon juice and pour into a jug for serving.

Carve the chicken, spoon some stuffing onto each plate and drizzle over some of the sauce. Serve with the potato boulangère and some vegetables of your choice.

POTATO BOULANGÈRE

4 onions
2 tabsp olive oil
750g potatoes, such as Roosters, peeled
300ml stock
drizzle of olive oil over the top
8 sage leaves

EQUIPMENT: Ovenproof dish about 23cm x 20 cm

Chop the onions in half and slice finely crossways. Heat the olive oil in a medium pot and add the onions. Season with salt, stir and cover with a butter paper or a circle of parchment paper placed directly on top of the onions. Sweat the onions slowly for about 20 minutes, stirring regularly, until completely tender and translucent. Remove from the heat.

Preheat the oven to 200°C, 180°C Fan, 350°F, Gas 6.

Slice the potatoes about 0.5cm thick. Butter the ovenproof dish on the base and the sides and overlap a third of the potatoes on the bottom of the dish. Season with salt. Shred the sage leaves and scatter half the sage and half the onions over the potatoes. Place another layer of overlapping potatoes on top, season and cover with the remaining onions and sage. Finish with the final layer of potatoes. Pour over hot stock until it almost comes up to the level of the potatoes. Drizzle a little olive oil over the surface and place in a preheated oven for about 45 minutes. After the first fifteen minutes or so, press the potatoes down with a spatula so that they remain flat.

In the final phase of cooking, say for the last 15 minutes, you may turn up the heat to 220°C, 200°C Fan, 425°F, Gas 7 to get more colour on the surface of the potatoes, if necessary. If all of the liquid has not evaporated but the potatoes are tender and golden, very gently tip the dish, holding back the potatoes. Pour off the remaining stock and reserve for the sauce.

NOTE For the potato boulangère, you could use chopped thyme or rosemary instead of the sage.

SPICES

SPICES

I find it quite grounding to go and seek out a food market when I am in a foreign city. I can browse and enquire and engage. My senses are awakened and I feel connected to the life of the place. If I anticipate the chance to do some cooking myself, then the banter around the stalls will be all the better. I will grab some vegetables and perhaps some meat or fish, or whatever appeals. I won't be burdened by a shopping list as I will have packed half a dozen spices, some whole and some ground, at the bottom of my case. These will work their particular magic on my purchases. This is what I love about spices: they can turn the most modest of ingredients into a feast fit for a king. The process of cooking with them also brings joy to my soul. I have always envied musicians who can jam together, heading towards a sound yet to be heard. This is how I feel when I bring out my spices. The only certainty is that this dish will not taste exactly as I have ever cooked it before. I am now the jazz improvisor, taking a bit of this and a bit of that and bringing those flavour-notes together in harmony. After a day's tramping the streets, this feeling of undaunted creativity will re-energise me. My senses will thrill as the aromas are released, the colours change and the flavours develop. I am not proposing that you pack your spices when you travel but the hope is that you can develop the confidence to improvise at home. Leave me the folly of bringing my little sachets with me. They are an insurance policy against the possibility of eating-out disappointments. They are my foreign currency.

THE JOY OF COOKING WITH
FRESH SPICES

If you are unused to cooking with fresh spices then it is surely time to get to grips with one of the great culinary traditions. The recipes can initially seem a little daunting and the techniques may be unfamiliar. My approach is to start this chapter with two foundation curries. They have certain ingredients and techniques in common and certain ingredients and techniques that mark them apart. I urge you to try both (not at the same time!) because the level of detail given for these curries will give you a really solid grounding for the later recipes. Each has its own simple accompaniments.

Shopping list

If you would like a shopping list for every recipe in this chapter, these are the spices that you will need.

If you see something a little more unusual like fresh curry leaves (not the dried ones), you could scoop up a big bunch. If transport is not too far away, you could also pick up a large bag of the best basmati rice.

If you wish to roast and grind spices to make your own garam masala (see page 248), the extra spices that are required are listed below.

coriander seeds
cumin seeds
cloves
chilli flakes
dried red chillies
Kashmiri chilli powder, available
  here under the brand Deggi Mirch
cinnamon sticks
ground cinnamon
black mustard seeds
black peppercorns
green cardamom pods
turmeric (ground)
saffron threads
tamarind
chaat masala
fenugreek leaves

garam masala - a combination of
  ground spices (though homemade
  is preferable)

EXTRA SPICES FOR
HOMEMADE GARAM MASALA
black cardamom pods
mace
nutmeg

Let's take spices slowly

This chapter is about getting to grips with the wonderful rituals and methods of coaxing out flavour from whole and freshly ground spices and becoming confident about ways in which they can be harmonised. There are a few general points to be made.

Purchasing a spice grinder

Your life will be made easier with a spice grinder. My current favourite is a Cuisinart model which comes with two detachable stainless steel containers. It's a modest investment. I use it for grinding spices as well as for making ginger and garlic pastes but I don't challenge it too much by putting in great lumps of ginger. The motor will simply become overheated. It's best to grate the ginger first on a microplane, to crush the garlic and to chop any other ingredients very finely. Two containers allow me to grind spices in one and make a paste in the other. A useful tip is to grind some stale bread (or uncooked white rice) in them after use. This is the simplest way to absorb any residual oils.

Where to buy spices

The second task is to work out where you are going to buy your spices. Your options are to find a local Asian market with a good turnover or to use an online source. Either option will mean that you can get spices easily and avoid the tiny, expensive supermarket jars. There is no need to buy vast amounts. Much can be done with half a dozen spices. I have noted that the best Indian chefs I have worked with use no more than ten spices when they are cooking at home. Since each one can be used in different ways, the possible combinations are already more than sufficient.

Learn the techniques

The third area is about learning the techniques. This is the chapter to cast off any fear about working with spices. Learn how to draw out their flavours and the variety of ways in which they can be combined. There is a special section on "key techniques" to which you can keep returning as a reference point.

Labelling your spice jars

Lastly, working with spices demands a degree of organisation. This is an area in which the ritual is far more pleasurable if you are not fumbling around in unmarked plastic bags, puzzling over the contents. A spice box makes your life easy because it is designed for this purpose. However, it is not essential: labelled jam jars or small containers work perfectly well. This then helps when you gather the spices for a particular recipe. You are well positioned to set out the whole spices, roast and grind others and measure those that are pre-ground. Laying out your spices is a good ritual and helps to ensure that your focus is where it needs to be.

KEY TECHNIQUES

Roasting & grinding cumin & coriander

Cumin and coriander seeds are the most commonly used in this chapter. They can be bought pre-ground but it's a better option to buy the seeds and to grind them. Better still is to toast the seeds to release their fragrance and then grind them. This is a wonderful ritual.

Place a bowl beside the cooker and pre-heat the pan for a couple of minutes. Add the coriander seeds in a single layer and roast over a medium heat, shaking or stirring the pan so that the seeds toast evenly. After a few minutes, the seeds will emit a sweet nutty aroma and they will start to go a shade darker. Pour them immediately into the bowl and allow to cool before grinding.

Add the cumin seeds to the pan. As these are very fine, they will toast even more quickly. Follow the same procedure, tossing them frequently until they release a toasted aroma which will be a feast for the senses. When they go a shade darker, whip them off the heat and pour into the bowl. Allow to cool before grinding.

Garam masala

In so many Indian households, garam masala is a guarded secret. It is a combination of anything between 10 and 20 spices that are roasted and ground to a powder and add their own unique flavour to dishes. Sometimes garam masala is used during the cooking process but more often it is added at the end to give that extra depth of flavour. Garam masala is available in all Asian shops but it would be made up of spices which would be ground but not roasted. If you have gone to the trouble of buying your own spice grinder, then why not take the plunge and roast and

grind your own. You should go the extra mile, particularly as I have gone to the trouble of asking my favourite Indian chef, Sunil Ghai, for his own family recipe. So here it is:

Makes 1 cup garam masala

50g cumin seeds
15g coriander seeds
12g black cardamom pods
8g green cardamom pods
3 tsp black peppercorns
5 sticks cinnamon
4g cloves
4g mace
4 large bay leaves
half a nutmeg

Heat a frying pan and add all the spices above. Toast over the heat, shaking the pan until they go a shade darker and emit a toasted aroma. Pour onto a sheet of parchment paper and allow to cool. Grind to a powder in a spice grinder. Label it "Sunil's Garam Masala" and don't tell anyone the secret.

Heat in Indian cooking

Cooking with a whole range of spices has come to be synonymous with heat but it is important to understand that there is a clear distinction between the two. Spices are added for flavour and depth, heat comes from adding chillies, in one form or another, or black pepper. Whether you add a little or a lot of heat is entirely in your control. For all my Indian cooking, I use Kashmiri chilli powder which is sold under the brand name Deggi Mirch, fondly known in our house as Deggi. These are mild ground chillies from Kashmir which add flavour and colour. The measures suggested for chilli powder throughout this book are for this brand. Other brands of chilli powder will vary in intensity and can come with additional spices added so check the labelling. Chilli powder gives instant heat so, particularly if you are using another brand, err on the side of caution. It is very easy to add more.

Mustard seeds

If you like a little entertainment as you cook, then mustard seeds will bring a smile to your face. When adding them to hot oil, they are generally added first because they start jumping up and down, like popcorn. The popping of the seeds releases their flavour. They are very mild and yet so distinctive. They will keep cropping up throughout this chapter so you will become very familiar with them.

Curry leaves

There are certain ingredients that I would make a special detour to buy. This is one of them. They are available in bunches and can just be picked off as required. Any not used can be refrigerated. After a day or two, if you are not planning to use them they would be better off in the freezer where they keep well. Store in an airtight container, not a ziplock bag which risks getting banged around. The leaves blacken easily if left out for any length of time, so sneak as many as you like out of the freezer but return the remainder straight away.

How to use tamarind

Tamarind is a fruit and the main souring agent in Asian cooking (adding a squeeze of lemon juice is a good alternative). The tamarind pods are peeled, semi-dried and compacted into blocks resembling a pack of stoned dates. They are available in Asian markets and can be stored in a cupboard, ready to be reconstituted. Be sure not to buy tamarind concentrate.

To use, simply tear off a piece of tamarind, place it in a small jug or bowl and cover with a similar amount of warm water. It's best to make the tamarind water quite thick so be careful not to add too much water or it will be too runny. Leave it to soften for 10 or 15 minutes and then mash with the back of a spoon and strain, discarding the fibres and any seeds. What remains is referred to as either tamarind pulp or tamarind water. Taste it. It has a lovely sweet and sour lemony flavour and will hold in the fridge for about 5 days.

Cooking whole spices in oil

One of the fascinating techniques in Indian cooking is frying whole spices in some oil before adding the other ingredients. It is important to understand that adding whole spices to hot oil releases their natural flavours - bringing the temperature of the oil up gradually does not have the same effect. To ensure that the oil is sufficiently hot, the trick is to drop in a single spice and see how it behaves. A green cardamom pod, for instance, will sizzle gently when it hits the oil and will puff up and brown in a few seconds. This will help to build layers of flavour. If the oil in the pan starts smoking before you begin the process, then remove the pan from the heat to allow the oil to cool down. Smoking oil will burn spices instantly. If you do burn spices, please throw them out and start again – always.

Tadka

Tadka is another process in which different herbs, spices or aromatics are added to hot oil. The difference here is that once the essence of the flavours have been released, the oil is poured over a finished dish (rather than being the starting point for adding other ingredients). It is often the vital last step in making a dal but it is a method used for adding depth and an enticing aroma to many other dishes.

Garlic & ginger paste

Ginger and garlic are key ingredients for so many of these recipes. It works well to crush the garlic and then to grate the ginger finely (a microplane is my favourite tool for the job) but a common technique is to make up a garlic and ginger paste. This has two advantages. You can get a smoother result in this way and you can have the paste ready for all the recipes at once and can refrigerate any you do not use for another day. The usual proportions favour 60% ginger and 40% garlic. It is easy to whizz up if you have a small blender. Peel the garlic and ginger. Chop them up roughly and whizz in the blender with a dash of water and sunflower oil. Purée to a paste, scraping down the sides every so often. The paste will oxidise unless kept covered and so press it into a jar and cover with a layer of oil.

LAMB KHEEMA

Kheema means ground meat or mince. The Indian name sounds so much more exotic, but this is simple fare, although very tasty. It's a perfect dish with which to start your own spice trail. If you want to be more ambitious at a later point, lamb kheema would make a great filling for a samosa but here I suggest that it might be served with Bombay Aloo potatoes and some simply cooked basmati rice. If this is your first dish with fresh spices, relish the process.

Serves 4

3 tbsp oil
1 onion, finely chopped
50g fresh ginger, finely chopped
5 cloves garlic, crushed
1 tsp ground cumin
1 tsp ground coriander

½ tsp turmeric
½ tsp Kashmiri chilli powder
   (Deggi Mirch brand)

100g Greek yoghurt
200g cherry tomatoes, chopped
600g minced lamb (not too lean)
2 tsp garam masala, bought
   or homemade

120g peas, fresh or frozen
1 small green chilli, deseeded
   and finely chopped
2 tbsp lemon juice
1 small bunch fresh
   coriander, chopped

The first step is to get your spices ready. You may have bought ground cumin and coriander but hopefully you will have bought the seeds so that you can grind them yourself. If your ambition is boundless, you might go to the techniques page and roast them before grinding. What an extraordinary start that would be.

Heat the oil in a casserole pot and add the onion. Season with salt and cook on a low heat with a lid on until softened, about 10 minutes. Add the ginger and garlic and stir for a few minutes. Mix in the cumin, coriander, turmeric and chilli powder and a dash of water and cook, while stirring, for another couple of minutes. The water helps prevent the ground spices from burning. Now pull the pan off the heat and add the yoghurt, one tablespoon at a time, to prevent it from splitting. When each spoonful is fully incorporated, add another. Mix in the chopped tomatoes and return the pot to the heat. Cook for about 5 minutes and then add in the minced lamb and garam masala. Season with salt and toss the meat around over a high heat until it becomes coloured. Pour in 250ml water, bring up to the boil and cover with a lid. Simmer for about 25 minutes until the lamb is tender.

Mix in the peas, green chilli, lemon juice and coriander and cook for a further 5 minutes. Taste and adjust the seasoning.

BOMBAY ALOO POTATOES
BASIC RAITA

Potatoes are seen as just another vegetable in Indian cooking. You could use leftover potatoes chopped into chunks, but cooking potatoes from scratch means that they absorb more flavour. It is so interesting to try out different spices with potatoes. This is one of my favourite combinations.

This recipe introduces black mustard seeds, which are a very mild yet distinctive spice and the extraordinarily aromatic curry leaves which are available in Asian markets but keep well in the freezer. If you do not have access to fresh curry leaves, then simply leave them out. Dried curry leaves are not an option.

Serves 4

BASIC RAITA
200g Greek yoghurt
pinch salt
pinch sugar
a few drops of lemon juice

FOR THE POTATOES
3 tbsp oil
500g potatoes
1 tsp black mustard seeds
12 fresh curry leaves (or frozen, but
   never dried)
1 onion, finely chopped

¼ tsp turmeric
1 tsp ground coriander
¼ tsp Kashmiri chilli powder
   (Deggi Mirch brand)

100ml water, or as needed
bunch of coriander,
   roughly chopped

To make the raita, simply mix all the ingredients together.

Chop the potatoes into cubes about 2cm square. Heat the oil in a medium saucepan. Drop 2 or 3 mustard seeds into the pot. They should sizzle as soon as they hit the oil. When the oil is hot enough, add the rest of the seeds. When they pop and crackle, drop in the curry leaves. Sauté for about 10 seconds and enjoy the drama and the extraordinary aroma that they emit. Mix in the onions, season with salt and cook, stirring regularly for at least 5 minutes or until the onions begin to soften.

Add the turmeric, ground coriander, chilli powder and a dash of water and cook out the spices for about 30 seconds, stirring as you go. Ground spices can burn very easily so as a matter of course, it is useful to keep a little jug of water beside you. Mix in the cubed potatoes, season with salt and add 100ml water. Continue cooking the potatoes with the lid on, stirring every so often, until they are barely tender. Add in more water as you go along if the mixture becomes too dry. At the end, adjust the seasoning. Finish with a bunch of chopped coriander.

Bombay Aloo potatoes are delicious served with the Lamb Kheema and a simple raita.

CHICKEN CURRY
TOMATOES
COCONUT MILK

This is a truly wonderful chicken curry. The coconut milk produces a quite different result. If you are approaching these recipes in order, you will be an old hand at some of the key techniques by now.

Serves 4-6

4 cardamom pods

3 cloves

1 dried red chilli

1 stick cinnamon

2-3 tbsp sunflower oil

1 onion, finely chopped

2 green or 1 red chilli

6 cloves garlic, crushed to a paste

1 tbsp finely grated ginger
  (or 2 tbsp garlic ginger paste)

2 tsp ground coriander

2½ tsp ground cumin

½ tsp turmeric

½ tsp Kashmiri chilli powder
  (Deggi Mirch brand)

1 x 400g tin coconut milk

1 x 400g tin chopped tomatoes

10 chicken thighs, without skin

finely chopped coriander, to add
  at the end

This recipe uses some ground spices and some whole spices. It is best to measure out your ground spices first, following the suggestion for roasting and grinding the coriander and cumin seeds outlined in the techniques section.

Place the whole spices in a little bowl. Heat the oil in a deep frying pan or casserole pot. Test the temperature of the oil by dropping in a single cardamom pod and watching it sizzle. Add the whole spices and after about 10 seconds, when the cloves and the cardamom pods puff up, add the onion. Season with salt and turn the heat down to low. Cover with a lid and sweat the onion until it has softened, about 10 minutes. Stir a few times during the cooking process.

Split the chillies in half, remove the seeds and chop finely. Add to the pot along with the garlic and ginger. Stir for a minute or two before mixing in the coriander, cumin, turmeric and chilli powder along with a dash of water. Season the chicken thighs with salt and place in the pan. Cook for a few minutes, turning them once or twice to coat them in the spices. Pour the coconut milk and tinned tomatoes into the pan and bring up to the boil.

Cover with a lid and transfer to a preheated oven for about 40 minutes. Cook until the chicken is tender and the meat comes easily away from the bone. (The chicken may also be cooked on the hob, if preferred). If the sauce is too runny, reduce it down by boiling to concentrate the flavour. Sprinkle over some chopped coriander.

NOTE If you wish to use a combination of thighs, legs and breasts, follow the same method as above but remove the chicken breasts from the sauce after about 20 minutes (depending on the thickness). Return them to the pot shortly before serving just to reheat through.

GOAN PRAWN CURRY

Goan cuisine is synonymous with seafood and though the spicing may vary, there are many elements here that are quite typical, namely the use of coconut milk, curry leaves and tamarind. The tadka, which is the infused oil poured over at the last minute, can also be perfumed with curry leaves.

Serves 4, or 6 as part of a spread

2 tbsp sunflower oil

½ tsp black mustard seeds

12 curry leaves

1 onion, thinly sliced

2 cloves garlic, finely chopped

1 tbsp ginger, finely chopped

2 small green chillies, sliced in half,
  seeds left in

1 dried red chilli

½ tsp paprika

½ tsp turmeric

1 tsp ground coriander

½ tsp ground cumin

pinch ground cinnamon

2 whole tomatoes, from a tin,
  roughly chopped

10 cherry tomatoes,
  roughly chopped

20 jumbo prawns

1 x 400g tin coconut milk

1 tbsp plus 2 tsp thick tamarind
  water, or more as required
  (see page 249)

TADKA

2-3 tbsp sunflower or coconut oil

6 curry leaves

1 green chilli, sliced in half

1 small round shallot, thinly sliced
  (or half a large one)

To prepare the curry

Heat the oil in a frying pan and when hot, add the black mustard seeds and curry leaves. The mustard seeds should sizzle and pop. After about 10 seconds, add the onions. Season with salt and sauté for about 5-8 minutes, stirring regularly, until the onions are tender and lightly coloured. Mix in the chopped garlic, ginger and green chillies and sauté for a further minute. Add the dried red chilli, the ground spices and a good dash of water and cook, stirring, for a further minute. Add the tinned tomatoes, cherry tomatoes and 100ml water and simmer for about 5 minutes until the tomatoes soften. Season the prawns with salt before combining with the sauce, turning them over a few times so that they become immersed in the liquid. Pour in the coconut milk and 1 tablespoon of tamarind water and continue to simmer for a further 5 minutes. Taste the sauce, check the seasoning and add a couple more teaspoons of tamarind water if some extra freshness is required. The prawn curry can be made up to this point in advance.

The tadka is poured over the curry just before serving.

To make the tadka

Heat the oil in a small frying pan or saucepan and when hot, add the curry leaves and chillies. After a few seconds, add the shallots and sauté for a few minutes until tender. Pour over the prawn curry and serve immediately.

ALMOND LAMB CURRY

For several years Atul Kochhar, the first Indian chef to gain a Michelin star, was a regular visitor to Dublin Cookery School. He would fly over from his London base early on a Saturday and cook with us for the day before flying home. Such are the demands on his time, we knew that this could not go on forever and so we relished his gentle presence. This is one of his recipes that has been on our menu ever since.

Serves 4-6

2-4 tbsp sunflower oil
800g boned lamb shoulder, cut
    into 4cm pieces
100g blanched almonds
2 tsp poppy seeds

30g tamarind pulp

2 tbsp sunflower oil
3 cloves
2 cinnamon sticks
4 green cardamom pods
10 curry leaves (if available)
2 medium onions or 1 Spanish
    onion, finely chopped
2 tbsp ginger garlic paste
    (or 3 cloves garlic, crushed &
    1 tbsp finely grated ginger)
½ tsp turmeric
3 tsp ground coriander
½-1 tsp Kashmiri chilli powder,
    (Deggi Mirch brand)
100ml tinned chopped tomatoes
    with juice

300ml chicken stock or water
salt
coriander leaves, to garnish

Heat a frying pan or casserole pot and add a couple tablespoons of oil. Season the lamb pieces and sear in batches over a high heat until golden on all sides. Do not overcrowd the pan or the lamb will stew rather than caramelise. Remove the lamb and set aside. Continue with the remaining pieces, searing them at a high temperature.

In a mini food processor or spice grinder, blend the almonds and poppy seeds to a paste. Place the tamarind in a small jug and pour over about 100ml warm water. Leave to soak for about 20 minutes. Mash the pulp with a spoon until it starts dissolving into the water. Push through a sieve, reserving the tamarind water. Discard the seeds and the fibrous pulp in the sieve.

Heat the oil in a deep pan. When hot, add the whole spices and the curry leaves. The spices should crackle when they hit the oil. After a few seconds, add the chopped onions, season with salt and cook over a medium heat until the onions soften. Stir the onions regularly and continue cooking until the onions turn golden brown. Add the ginger garlic paste (or crushed garlic and grated ginger) and cook, stirring, for 2-3 minutes to cook out the rawness of the paste.

Add the turmeric, coriander and the chilli powder to the pot along with the tinned tomatoes and stock or water. Mix in the ground nuts and poppy seeds and the seared lamb. Stir to mix and then bring up to the boil. Place a lid on the pot and transfer to a preheated oven for about 1-1¼ hours. If the sauce becomes a little too thick during the cooking, add extra water or stock. The lamb shoulder should be meltingly tender at the end. Stir in one tablespoon of tamarind water. Taste and adjust the seasoning. To serve, garnish with the coriander. The curry may be prepared a day or two in advance and reheated.

CAULIFLOWER KORMA
PEAS & RAISINS

Some Indian restaurants have churned out disappointing kormas which have somewhat tarnished the reputation of this dish. This delicate curry reinstates it as the food of emperors. It is enriched by the creamy texture of the cashews, subtle spicing and the surprise hit, the plump juicy raisins which add a burst of sweetness.

Serves 4-6

1 cauliflower
about 20 saffron threads

60g unsalted cashews
3 whole green cardamom pods
2 tsp coriander seeds
1 tsp cumin seeds
5cm cinnamon stick

2.5 cm piece ginger, finely chopped
2 large cloves garlic, chopped
2 green chillies, chopped (one
　with seeds)

2-3 tbsp sunflower oil
2 cloves
1 onion, finely chopped
100ml Greek yoghurt
200-400ml water or
　Marigold bouillon
45g raisins (giant if possible)
70g frozen or fresh peas
½ tsp garam masala
squeeze of lemon juice
chopped fresh coriander, to finish

Cut the cauliflower into large florets, about 3cm across, making sure to keep the root end intact. The exact size is not important but try and keep them all a similar size. Soak the saffron in 4 tablespoons of boiling water for 10 minutes.

To make the nut & spice paste
Grind the nuts finely and remove. Place the cardamom, coriander, cumin and cinnamon in a spice grinder and grind to a powder. Remove. Place the ginger, garlic and chillies in a blender and whizz to a fine paste, adding about 50-100ml water. Mix the ginger and chilli paste with the cashews and ground spices.

To cook the korma
Heat the oil in a deep frying pan. When hot, add the cloves, leave for about 10-15 seconds until they swell and then add the onions. Season with salt, stir and place a lid on the pan. Allow to sweat for 10 minutes until they are tender and translucent. Add the spice paste to the onions and stir regularly for about 5 minutes over a low heat, adding a splash of water if necessary. Pull the pan off the heat and add one tablespoon of yoghurt to the pan, stirring until it is incorporated. Repeat with the rest of the yoghurt, adding 1 tablespoon at a time.

Return the pan to the heat, pour in 200ml water and bring up to the boil. Mix in the cauliflower florets and season generously with salt. Pour in the saffron and its soaking water and scatter over the raisins. Simmer gently, with a lid on, for about 10 minutes, turning the cauliflower every so often, until it is tender but still with a bite. Be careful not to overcook it at this point. Add more water to the sauce if it is reducing too much. Scatter over the peas and cook for a further couple of minutes. Finish by sprinkling in the garam masala, check for seasoning and add a squeeze of lemon juice. Garnish with some chopped coriander.

LEG OF LAMB
SPICED YOGHURT
CARROT & SULTANA RAITA

I love my cookery books dearly and some have long and personal histories. One of these is my first spice book, a battered copy of Madhur Jaffrey's *Indian Cooking*. As an actress who came to London in the 1970s, she would regularly write letters home for her much-missed family recipes. These were turned into a TV series and an accompanying book which went on to sell half a million copies. I met her in New York twenty years later and she asked me whether I still cooked any of these recipes. I was able to rattle them off. This is one, slightly adapted, in which a leg of lamb is marinated, ideally for at least 24 hours. You could make half the marinade for a smaller leg. With a large one, make sure to ask the butcher to remove the aitch bone at the top of the leg. Also ask him to chop the very end of the leg close to the meat so that it will fit in the roasting dish snugly. Attempting to hatchet if off yourself is not a great idea. I know, I have tried.

There are many options to accompany this lamb dish. I love a saucy vegetable, such as the chickpea masala, as well as the crunchy green beans with black mustard seeds.

Serves 6

2.25kg leg of lamb

SPICED YOGHURT MARINADE
220g onions, coarsely chopped
6 cloves garlic
4 x 2.5cm pieces ginger, chopped
3 fresh green chillies, seeds left
  in and coarsely chopped
2 tbsp ground cumin
1½ tbsp ground coriander
½ tsp Kashmiri chilli powder
½ tsp garam masala
50g ground almonds
600ml Greek yoghurt
3 tsp salt

TEMPERING SPICES
4 tbsp sunflower oil
6 whole cloves
16 cardamom pods
10 black peppercorns
2 x 5 cm sticks cinnamon

carrot and sultana raita, see overleaf

Remove any fat from the outside of the leg of lamb as well as any parchment type skin. With a small utility knife, cut a few gashes over the top and underside of the lamb.

To marinate the lamb
In a blender, whizz the onions, garlic, ginger and chillies until puréed to a fine paste. Mix in the marinade spices and the ground almonds. Place the yoghurt and salt in a bowl and add the spice paste. Place the lamb snugly into a dish. Rub the paste into the gashes and all over the top and underside of the lamb . There is a lot of marinade but the excess will be used as a pouring sauce. Cover the dish in clingfilm and place the lamb in the fridge for up to 24 hours. Allow the lamb to come to room temperature about 1 hour before cooking.

To cook the lamb
Preheat the oven to 200°C, 180°C fan, 400°F, Gas 6.

Heat the oil in a frying pan and when hot, add the cloves, cardamom pods, black peppercorns and cinnamon. Leave for about 10 seconds to allow the cloves to swell and then pour the contents of the pan over the lamb. Cover the lamb with foil and place in a preheated oven for about 45 minutes. Remove the foil, baste the lamb and return it to the oven for a further 20-30 minutes. The exact timing will depend on the size of the leg. If you have a meat thermometer, a temperature of about 54°C-57°C / 130°F-135°F is ideal for medium rare lamb. Allow the lamb to rest for about 15 minutes before carving.

Turn the remaining lamb and yoghurt crust into the most wonderful lamb patties...

Sweat a large onion in 1 tablespoon of oil until tender and translucent. Mix in some ground cumin and coriander, say a teaspoon of each, along with a dash of water. Cook this out for a minute or so. Whizz the meat in a food processor until fairly fine but still with some texture. Pour into a bowl, add a handful of breadcrumbs and the onions. If you have any sauce left from some of the accompaniments you served with the lamb such as the chickpea masala, a few spoonfuls can be a great addition. If not, then add a little beaten egg to moisten. Season with salt, mix well and form it into patties with your hands. Just before serving, dunk the top and bottom of each patty in plain flour or gram flour, shake off the excess, then dip into beaten egg and finely into some breadcrumbs to coat the surface. Panfry in oil until golden on both sides. Serve with the raita below.

CARROT & SULTANA RAITA

300g natural yoghurt

¼ tsp salt

¼ tsp Kashmiri chilli powder
   (Deggi Mirch brand)

1 tsp honey

2 small carrots, peeled and
   coarsely grated

1-2 tbsp sunflower oil

½ tsp cumin seeds

½ tsp black mustard seeds

30g sultanas

Place the yoghurt in a bowl and mix with the salt, chilli powder, and honey. Stir in the carrots. Heat the oil in a small saucepan or frying pan and when hot, add the cumin and mustard seeds. When the mustard seeds start popping, add in the sultanas and mix around. Pour the spice and sultana mix over the yoghurt.

CHAPATTIS

You can buy ready-made chapattis in Asian markets but you would miss out on the real pleasure of making them, as well as the superior result. It is hard to imagine a more basic bread. This is just flour, water and a little seasoning. Roll them out into a round and put them on a frying pan or cast-iron griddle and watch them blister and speckle in the heat. They would usually be served as a bread on the side. However, I also love them rolled around a selection of ingredients, such as the lamb koftas overleaf, and eaten in the hand.

Makes 8 chapattis

250g chapatti flour
½ tsp salt
120ml-150ml water, or more
  if required
extra flour for rolling
2 tbsp melted butter, for brushing
  over the chapattis

To make the dough
Mix the flour and salt in a bowl. Pour in about 120ml water and mix together, adding some more water if required to yield a soft dough. Turn out onto a floured surface and knead for a few minutes. Return the dough to the bowl, cover with clingfilm and allow to rest for about 15 minutes or longer.

Shaping, rolling & cooking the chapattis
Divide the dough into 8 pieces. Shape them into balls. On a floured surface, flatten each piece with the palm of your hand and then roll out into a disc of about 12cm. Heat a flat cast-iron frying pan, griddle or non-stick frying pan. When hot, place one of the circles of dough on the pan and cook over a low to medium heat for 1-2 minutes until bubbles appear on the surface. Check the underside of the chapatti. It should be speckled with brown marks. Turn over and repeat on the other side. If you wish to make the breads in advance, wrap in tinfoil and keep warm in the oven. If you wish to serve the breads straight away and you are working on a gas hob, then try this extra magical step after cooking the chapatti on the pan. Using a tongs, hold each chapatti over the gas flame for a few seconds. The bread will puff up dramatically. Brush with a little melted butter and devour while still warm.

NO CHAPATTI FLOUR? NO PROBLEM.

Either use all wholewheat flour which has been sieved to remove the bran flakes or use a combination of half wholewheat and half white flour instead of the chapatti flour.

CHAPATTIS, LAMB KOFTAS
CARROT & MUSTARD SEED SALAD
MINT & CORIANDER CHUTNEY

My first choice of fillings for these chapattis are koftas or spicy meatballs. The spices are added to the minced meat and the small orbs are formed easily with slightly wet hands. You could easily imagine them in their own curry sauce but here they are served with grated carrots, mustard seeds and a mint and coriander chutney and then packed into the chapatti.

Serves 4-6
Makes about 30 koftas

LAMB KOFTAS
600g lamb mince
1 tsp ground cumin
1 tsp ground coriander
1 tsp chilli powder
2 tsp ground ginger
2 tsp garam masala
2 cloves garlic, crushed
2 tbsp mint, chopped
2 tbsp chopped coriander
½ tsp salt
oil, for frying

CARROT & MUSTARD SEED SALAD
350g carrots, peeled and grated
   coarsely
¼ tsp salt
2 tbsp oil
1 tbsp whole black mustard seeds
1 tbsp lemon juice

chapattis, freshly made (see
   previous page) or bought
mint & coriander chutney (see
   overleaf)
red onion and pomegranate
   salad (see overleaf)

Preheat the oven to 180°C, 160°C Fan, 350°F, Gas 4.

To prepare the koftas
Place all the ingredients for the meatballs together in a bowl and blend with your hands. Shape into small round meatballs. Heat 2 tablespoons of oil in a large frying pan and add the meatballs. Sear on all sides and then transfer the pan to a preheated oven for about 5 minutes for the koftas to cook through. The timing will depend on their size. Remove from the oven and keep warm.

To make the carrot salad
Place the carrots in a bowl and season with salt. Heat the oil in a small pan, and when hot, add the mustard seeds. As soon as the mustard seeds pop, pour the contents of the pan, oil and seeds over the carrots. Add the lemon juice and mix together.

Serve the chapattis with the carrot salad, koftas, mint and coriander chutney and the red onion and pomegranate salad, if using.

MINT & CORIANDER CHUTNEY

This is a fresh and vibrant chutney that could be served with a selection of Indian dishes.

45g mint leaves
45g coriander leaves
2 fresh green chillies, seeds
   left in one, roughly chopped
75g onion, roughly chopped
1½ tsp sugar
¼ tsp ground cumin
1 tbsp lime juice
salt
3-4 ice cubes (or 2 tbsp cold water)
150g Greek yoghurt

Place all the chutney ingredients, except for the yoghurt, in a food processor or blender and whizz to a rough paste. Mix in the yoghurt. Cover and refrigerate until ready to use. This chutney is best made on the day but will last for a couple of days.

RED ONION & POMEGRANATE SALAD

This red onion and pomegranate salad works well with the stuffed chapattis but would also be a good accompaniment to the chickpea burgers (see page 130) or the lamb burgers (see page 213).

2 red onions
pinch of salt
pinch of sugar
squeeze of lime juice

bunch of coriander, roughly chopped
small bunch of mint, roughly
   chopped
handful of pomegranate seeds
   (see page 154)

Chop the red onion in half and slice very thinly crossways. Place in a bowl, add a pinch of salt and sugar and a squeeze of lime juice. Mix and leave for about 15 minutes. Add in the pomegranate seeds and chopped herbs. Serve with the lamb koftas (see previous page).

SPINACH & CHICKPEA CAKES
MUSTARD & YOGHURT CHUTNEY

Sometimes I use my familiar ground coriander and ground cumin in this recipe but if I want something just a little more distinctive, I might use some chaat masala as well as some fenugreek leaves, both readily available in Asian markets. The other ingredients are easy to source, the mixture is satisfying to bring together and the patties are easily formed. I like to serve them on their own with a mustard and yoghurt chutney so that the subtlety of their taste can be fully appreciated, but they work equally well as one element of a meal.

Makes 6 x 6cm patties

300g frozen spinach

20g coriander

2 tbsp sunflower oil

1 tsp cumin seeds

50g ginger, very finely diced

2 large or 3 medium green chillies,
    seeds removed and very
    finely chopped

1 x 400g tin chickpeas, drained
    and rinsed

½ tsp ground coriander

1 tsp chaat masala

1 tsp fenugreek leaves

50g fresh spinach, roughly
    chopped

sunflower oil, for cooking

salt

gram flour (chickpea flour),
    for dipping

mustard and yoghurt chutney
    (see overleaf)

Defrost the spinach. If time is tight, you may put the spinach in a sieve and pour over some boiling water. When the spinach has defrosted, squeeze out the excess water. Chop the spinach roughly. Separate the stems and leaves from the coriander. Chop the stalks finely and keep the leaves for later.

Heat the oil in a pan and add the whole cumin seeds. Allow the spices to crackle for a few seconds (they will go a slight shade darker) and then add the ginger, green chilli, coriander stems and a pinch of salt. Sweat at a low to medium heat for about 5 minutes until the chilli and ginger have softened. Mix in the frozen spinach and the chickpeas. Crush the chickpeas with a fork so that they break down but still retain some texture. Sprinkle in the ground coriander, chaat masala, fenugreek leaves and the fresh spinach. Season with salt and then cook for about 5 minutes, stirring every so often to blend the ingredients together. Taste for seasoning and if the mixture needs a little more flavour, add extra chaat and fenugreek leaves. At the end, the excess moisture from the spinach will have evaporated. Spread out on a tray to cool.

When cold, scoop up a fistful of the mixture and compact with your hands into a patty about 6cm in diameter and 2cm thick. The size is not important. If the mixture is too wet, sprinkle in a couple of tablespoons gram flour (or potato flour) before shaping. These patties may be made in advance up to this point and refrigerated.

Just before cooking, dip the top and bottom of the spinach cakes into gram flour and shake off the excess. Heat 2-3 tablespoons of oil in the pan and when hot, add the patties to the pan. Cook on a medium heat until the underside goes golden, before turning over to repeat on

the other side, adding more oil if necessary. Serve with the mustard and yoghurt chutney.

If you wish to do a little more prep in advance, you could also panfry the spinach and chickpea cakes an hour or so before serving, remove them from the pan and place on a cold baking tray. They could then be warmed in a hot oven at 200°C, 180°C Fan, 400F, Gas 6.

NOTE   No chaat masala or fenugreek leaves? Then just use coriander and cumin as the two spices. Increase the ground coriander to 1 teaspoon and add ½ teaspoon of ground cumin instead of the fenugreek leaves.

MUSTARD & YOGHURT CHUTNEY

I love to have a fresh cooling yoghurt accompaniment to every spicy meal. This is the chutney I probably use most often. The use of the "tadka" makes it very special.

Serves 6

300g Greek yoghurt
¼ tsp salt

TADKA
1 tbsp sunflower oil
1 tsp mustard seeds
10 fresh or frozen curry leaves
   (optional)
½ tsp turmeric
1 tbsp honey
4 tsp lime juice

Place the yoghurt in a bowl and season with salt. Heat the oil in a pan and when hot, add the mustard seeds. They should sizzle as soon as they hit the oil and will then start popping and jumping. As soon as they quieten down, add the curry leaves and turmeric. The curry leaves will curl up from the heat of the oil. After about 10 seconds, pour the curried oil, along with all the spices, on top of the yoghurt and stir in. Add the honey and lime juice. If you find it a little sour add more honey, a little sweet add more lime juice. My own preference leans slightly to the sweet side.

CHICKPEA MASALA

Pickle restaurant is one of my favourite Indian restaurants in Dublin. I like to try different dishes on the menu but the one I will always order is their chickpea masala. I am sure that Sunil Ghai would give me the recipe but that would take away the enjoyment of eating it there. I generally see chickpeas as hearty and wholesome but with spices they really come alive. My attention is drawn to texture and taste that is often absent when they are unspiced. This is a very simple chickpea recipe with tinned chickpeas which I would happily just eat with rice and raita. It would not be out of place as part of a bigger spicy feast.

Serves 4 - 6

2 tabsp sunflower oil
1 large onion, finely chopped
salt
2 cloves garlic, crushed
1 tbsp ginger, finely chopped
2 green chillies, finely chopped,
   seeds left in
1 tabsp ground coriander
2 tsps ground cumin
½ tsp ground turmeric
½ tsp Kashmiri chilli powder
   (Deggi Mirch brand)
1 x 400g tin chopped tomatoes
2 x 400g tins chickpeas, drained
200ml water

TO FINISH
½ tsp garam masala
1-2 tbsp lemon juice
2.5cm piece ginger, peeled and
   cut into matchsticks
small bunch of chopped coriander,
   to serve

Heat the oil in a casserole pot and add the chopped onions. Season with salt, cover and cook over a medium heat, stirring regularly, until the onions are tender and translucent. Remove the lid and cook, stirring regularly, until the onions take on a bit of colour. Add the garlic, ginger and chillies and cook for another couple of minutes.

Mix in the ground coriander, cumin, turmeric, chilli power and a good dash of water and cook out the spices for a minute or two. Stir in the tomatoes and cook for about 10 minutes until the tomatoes start to break down. Add the tinned chickpeas, 200ml water and simmer for about 20 minutes or until the chickpeas have absorbed the flavour of the spices and the sauce is quite thick. The chickpeas may be prepared up to this point in advance, cooled and refrigerated. The final spicing should be added just before serving.

Add in the garam masala and lemon juice. Taste for seasoning and balance, perhaps adding a little more garam masala or lemon juice to produce a slightly bitter kick. Pour into a dish and garnish with chopped coriander and julienne of ginger.

KACHUMBER SALAD

This is one of the most popular Indian salads and there are variations in nearly every Indian cookbook. It is crunchy and cooling and works well with spicy food.

Serves 6

1 tsp cumin seeds
1 cucumber
10 cherry tomatoes
8 radishes
½ red onion, very finely diced
1 green chilli, deseeded and
    finely chopped
10 mint leaves, chopped
15g coriander leaves and stems,
    roughly chopped
2 tbsp lemon juice

Dry roast the cumin seeds in a small frying pan. To do this, simply preheat the pan and when hot, scatter on the cumin seeds. Allow the seeds to toast a little, shaking the pan every so often until they turn a shade darker. Remove immediately to a bowl and allow to cool.

Split the cucumber into quarters and remove the strip of seeds with a knife. Chop the rest of the cucumber into smallish chunks and place in a bowl. Quarter the cherry tomatoes. Slice the radish as thinly as possible. Add the red onion, chilli, mint and coriander. Grind the cumin seeds in a pestle and mortar. Season the salad with salt, add the lemon juice and sprinkle over the roasted cumin. Mix, taste for balance and seasoning and adjust as necessary.

CHANDANA'S CABBAGE
MUSTARD SEEDS & CURRY LEAVES

Chandana is a dear friend whose husband is a boarding school headmaster. I needn't tell you how eccentric the place is because a documentary maker has done that job for me in a recently released film (In Loco Parentis) which catches the atmosphere perfectly. I am not quite sure why, but the last time we cooked together we ended up in the school kitchen. It was freezing cold and all the pots were enormous, even all the implements seemed over-sized. We laughed our way through - a mixture of hilarity and hysteria. A bunch of people arrived for dinner and set up a table in the staff room which seemed half a mile down a dim corridor of uneven tiles. We piled a trolley high with our labours, trundled our way down and decided that we would not return for anything that we might have forgotten. The dish that outshone even the craziness of the evening was her cabbage with mustard seeds. I have cooked it numerous times since and it does not require such unique surroundings. Chandana's cabbage - East meets West.

1 head savoy cabbage
2-3 tbsp sunflower oil
1 tbsp black mustard seeds
12-14 curry leaves
½ tsp Kashmiri chilli powder
  (Deggi Mirch brand see page 248)
salt

Remove the dark green outer leaves from the cabbage and discard any that are damaged. Remove the thick central vein from the outer leaves. Slice the cabbage into quarters and remove the core. Sit each quarter on the chopping board and shred thinly crossways.

Heat a large frying pan and when hot, add the oil. Test the temperature by adding a few mustard seeds. They should sizzle quietly. Throw in the rest of the mustard seeds and heat until they start popping and jumping. At this point, toss in the curry leaves. They will spit a little as they hit the oil and curl up instantly. Slide the cabbage from the chopping board into the pan. Sprinkle over the chilli powder, season with salt and sauté over a medium heat until the cabbage starts to soften, adding a dash of water during the process. Toss the cabbage regularly over a medium heat until it has wilted but still retains some crunch. Check for seasoning and for heat. Another pinch of chilli powder may be just what it needs. If you are not serving the cabbage immediately, spread it out on a tray to cool quickly.

GREEN BEANS
BLACK MUSTARD SEEDS

I find it hard to put in words what impact mustard seeds have. The best way of appreciating their unique mildness is with something very simple. These green beans are transformed by their presence and I would be happy to serve them with any non-Indian dish. If you can find a word to do justice to mustard seeds and to describe their mystical effect, let me know.

Serves 4

450g green beans
4 tbsp vegetable oil
1 tbsp black mustard seeds
2 garlic cloves, finely chopped
1 hot dried red chilli, broken slightly
    so that it releases some of
    the seeds
1 tsp salt
½ tsp caster sugar

Blanch the beans in a pot of boiling water for 3–4 minutes, or until they are just tender but still with a nice bite. Drain immediately in a colander. If you are preparing the green beans in advance, plunge them directly into cold water, leave for a few minutes till cold and then drain. The beans may be blanched ahead of time.

Heat the oil in a large frying pan. When hot, add in the mustard seeds. As soon as they begin to pop, add the garlic and the red chilli. Stir for a few seconds. Put in the green beans, salt and sugar and stir to mix. Turn down the heat to low and cook the beans, stirring regularly for 7–8 minutes, until they have absorbed the flavour of the spices. Serve immediately.

SWISS CHARD
CORIANDER & TOASTED CASHEWS

I find it hard to pass by a bunch of Swiss chard. The leaves have such beauty, particularly if they have the red or yellow stems. I imagine that they have a slightly haughty air, even an arrogance, when they find themselves beside some spinach leaves but I don't begrudge them that: the crinkly leaves really are special. They are very easy to prepare with spices and a hint of heat from a chilli. If I want a contrast of texture, some cashew nuts can offer a little crunch.

sunflower oil, for cooking
2 tbsp cashews

400g Swiss chard (or spinach leaves)
¾ tsp coriander seeds
1 small dried red chilli
1 medium onion, finely sliced
1 clove garlic, chopped
10 small cherry tomatoes,
  roughly chopped
½ tsp ground turmeric
½ tsp garam masala
salt

Heat a small frying pan and add 2 teaspoons of sunflower oil. When hot, throw in the cashews and toss over the heat until they become toasted. Season with a pinch of salt and remove from the pan. Set aside until ready to use. Remove the ends of the Swiss chard stems, keeping them on the leaves unless they are very thick. Chop the stems into 2cm pieces.

Heat a frying pan and when hot, add the coriander seeds and chilli. Toast over the heat, for a minute or two, shaking the pan until the coriander seeds turn a shade darker. Remove from the heat. Crush in a pestle and mortar or whizz in a spice grinder to a powder.

Heat a dash of oil in a frying pan and add the sliced onions. Season with salt, place a lid on the pan and cook until tender. Add the chopped garlic and sauté for a minute before mixing in the coriander and chilli powder and a dash of water. Stir and cook briefly before mixing in the chopped tomatoes and turmeric. Cook on a low heat to soften the tomatoes.

Just before serving, add the stems of the chard and a dash of water. Tenderise the stems for a couple of minutes before mixing in the chard leaves. Toss until they wilt and season with salt. You may need to add a few tablespoons of water. Sprinkle in the garam masala and the toasted cashews and serve.

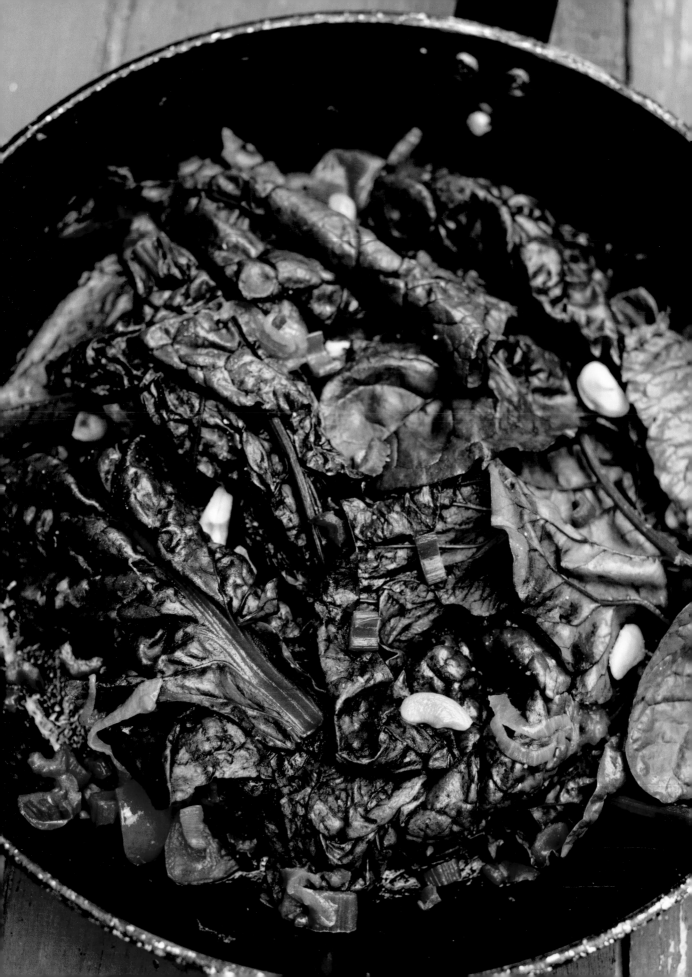

BASMATI RICE

Basmati rice has an aroma and flavour that is quite distinct. I often serve it plain as there may be so many spices in all the accompanying dishes. In India rice is graded for quality but, unfortunately, there is no grading system in the shops here. Look for long, slender unbroken grains and buy the best quality you can. In Asian markets there will be a dazzling choice of varieties compared to a regular supermarket.

FOOLPROOF BASMATI

If I am in a hurry to get supper on the go, this is the quickest method to cook rice. All I need is a shallot or onion, rice, salt and a little butter or oil. The rice cooks partly in the water and partly in the steam created by a tight-fitting lid. The quantity of water used here is 1½ times water to rice. If the lid on the saucepan is in any way loose, then put a piece of foil under the lid to seal it.

Serves 6

Basmati rice measured to the
  425ml level in a measuring jug
30g butter (or 1 tabsp sunflower oil)
1 large banana shallot or 3 small
  round shallots, finely chopped
650ml water
1 level tsp salt

Rinsing the rice
Basmati rice must always be rinsed thoroughly before cooking to remove the excess starch. Pour the rice into a bowl, cover with cold water and swirl around gently with your hands. The water will become cloudy from the starch. Let the rice settle to the bottom of the bowl for a few seconds. Then tilt the bowl and pour off the water, holding the rice back with one hand if necessary. Repeat this process 4 or 5 times until the water runs clear.

Cooking the rice
Choose an appropriate sized saucepan for the amount of rice. Heat the butter and add the shallot. Cook for a couple of minutes and then add the drained rice. Stir gently to coat the rice with the butter. Pour in the water and the salt and bring up to the boil. As soon as the water is bubbling, turn the heat down to the very lowest setting and place a lid on the pot. Don't peek at or stir the rice until the end of the cooking. After 15 minutes, remove the lid and part the grains of rice gently to see if all the water has evaporated. (This does not count as peeking). If there are still signs of water, carry on cooking for a few more minutes with the lid on. Taste a few grains of rice. If the water has evaporated before the rice is ready, add a couple more tablespoons and continue cooking with the lid on. Turn off the heat and leave it to sit for at least 5 minutes without disturbing. At the point of serving, fluff up the grains of rice with a fork. Cooked rice generally remains warm, covered with a lid, for up to half an hour.

BASMATI RICE WITH ATTITUDE

I would happily go into Sunil Ghai's restaurant, *Pickle*, just for a bowl of his "pilau" rice with some lentils. His understanding of rice is masterful and his recipe here produces the most incredible result with a heady fragrance and the flavour of fresh spices.

The whole spices are thrown into hot oil, onions are added and sautéed over a high heat and then the pre-soaked rice is added to the pot. The rice is covered with twice the amount of water and brought up to a really fast boil and left boiling away merrily until the water has reduced to the level of the rice. Sunil always places a damp teacloth on top of the rice at this point, to keep the moisture in and to help the rice to steam, but parchment paper will do the job nicely. At the end, the teacloth is whisked away and the rice can be fluffed up with a fork.

Serves 8

500g basmati rice
2 tbsp sunflower oil
a few knobs of butter

1 tsp cumin seeds
1 x 5cm stick cinnamon
1 tsp coriander seeds
5 cardamom pods

1 onion, finely chopped
1½ tsp salt
1 litre water, or less if you soak
    the rice for longer
coriander leaves, for garnish

Pour the rice into a bowl, cover with cold water and swirl around with your hands. The water will become cloudy from the starch. Let the rice settle to the bottom of the bowl for 2-3 seconds. Then tilt the bowl and pour off the water, holding the rice back with one hand if necessary. Repeat this process 4 or 5 times until the water runs clear. On the last occasion, cover the rice generously with water and leave to soak for 20-30 minutes. You may leave the rice for longer, in which case you will need to reduce the amount of water in which it is cooked. Drain through a sieve.

Place the whole spices in a little bowl beside the cooker. Heat the oil and a knob of butter and when hot, add in all the spices. They should sizzle when they hit the oil. After about 10 seconds, mix in the onions and sauté until they turn a light golden brown colour, stirring regularly. Pour in the rice and when coated with the butter and spices, add the salt and cold water. If the rice has been soaking for longer than 20 minutes, you will require less water – say about 800ml if it has been soaking for an hour.

Bring the water up to the boil and allow to boil until the water reduces down to the same level or just below the surface of the rice. Add a few knobs of butter on top and place a piece of parchment paper sitting directly on the rice. Cover with a lid and turn down the heat to very low. Continue cooking until the rice is tender, about 8 minutes. Remove the lid, check the grains and if they are tender, replace the lid and leave to sit until ready to serve. Fluff up the grains with a fork and place in a serving dish. Garnish with some coriander leaves.

PERSIAN RICE
CINNAMON ONIONS
PISTACHIOS & SULTANAS

I came across the title "Persian Rice" and have stuck with the name although I am not quite sure of its association. It is a festive rice but don't wait for the big occasion. Cook this when you have some friends in. The first thing that makes it stand apart is its wonderful yellow colour that comes from the saffron. Then there are a range of whole spices and it is finished with a garnish of both nuts and sultanas as well as the red onions cooked with cinnamon. Very special.

Serves 6

basmati rice measured to the 400ml
   level in a measuring jug

CINNAMON ONIONS
1 tbsp oil
2 red onions, halved and very
   thinly sliced
salt
½ tsp ground cinnamon
1 tsp brown sugar
1 red chilli, deseeded and
   finely chopped

TO GARNISH
handful of pistachios
handful of sultanas
1 tbsp sunflower oil

FOR THE RICE
½ tsp saffron threads, soaked in
   2 tbsp hot water
2 tbsp sunflower oil
½ cinnamon pod
3 green cardamom pods
3 cloves
1 bay leaf
10 peppercorns

To soak the rice
Place the rice in a bowl, cover with cold water and swirl the rice around gently with your hands. The water will become quite cloudy. Pour off the water and repeat this procedure about four times. Drain the rice and then cover with cold water and leave to sit for about 20 minutes or up to an hour. Drain the rice through a sieve.

For the cinnamon onions
Heat the oil and add the sliced onions. Season with salt, stir to mix and place a lid on the pot. Cook slowly, stirring regularly, until the onions are translucent. Remove the lid and continue cooking until the onions are becoming golden and a little crispy. Add the cinnamon, sugar and red chilli and cook for a few more minutes.

For the garnish
Heat the oil and when hot, add the pistachios. Toast for a few minutes in the oil and then add the sultanas. Heat until the sultanas puff up. Drain on kitchen paper.

To cook the rice
Place the saffron in a small bowl or jug. Soak in 4 tablespoons of boiling water.

Heat 2 tablespoons of oil in a medium sized pot. When hot, add the cinnamon, cardamom pods, cloves, bay leaf and peppercorns. Cook for about 20 seconds until the spices puff up a bit and then add the drained rice. Stir to coat the rice and then add 800ml cold water (a little less if the rice has soaked for an hour). Bring the rice up to the boil and continue to cook at a rolling boil until the water has reduced to the level of the rice.

At this point, place a piece of baking parchment directly on the rice and cover with a lid. Turn down the heat to its

very lowest setting and leave to cook for about another 8 minutes. Remove the lid and taste a few grains of rice. If the water has evaporated before the rice is ready, add a few more tablespoons and continue cooking with the lid on. Turn off the heat and leave to sit with the lid on for up to 15 minutes.

To serve

Fluff the rice with a fork and serve in a wide bowl garnished with the pistachios, sultanas and cinnamon onions.

WEIGHING & MEASURING

For consistency, I have used American tablespoon measurements throughout the book. American spoon measures are available in all kitchen stores or online.

All spoon measurements are level.

5ml = 1 teaspoon and 15ml = 1 tablespoon.

Where olive oil is referenced in this book, use only extra virgin oil.

Ounces to grams

OUNCES	GRAMS
½ oz	10 g
¾ oz	20 g
1 oz	25 g
1½ oz	40 g
2 oz	50 g
2½ oz	60 g
3 oz	75 g
4 oz	110 g
4½ oz	125 g
5 oz	150 g
6 oz	175 g
7 oz	200 g
8 oz	225 g
9 oz	250 g
10 oz	275 g
12 oz	350 g
1 lb	450 g
1 lb 8oz	700 g
2 lb	900 g
3 lb	1.35kg

Dimensions

INCHES	METRIC
1/8	3 mm
¼	5 mm
½	1 cm
¾	2 cm
1	2.5 cm
1¼	3 cm
1½	4 cm
1¾	4.5 cm
2	5 cm
2½	6 cm
3	7.5 cm
3½	9 cm
4	10 cm
5	13 cm
5¼	13.5 cm
6	15 cm
6½	16 cm
7	18 cm
7½	19 cm
8	20 cm
9	23 cm
9½	24 cm
10	25.5 cm
11	28 cm
12	30 cm
16	40 cm

Pints to Litres

IMPERIAL	METRIC
1 fl oz	25 ml
2 fl oz	50 ml
4 fl oz	100 ml
6 fl oz	175 ml
7 fl oz	200 ml
8 fl oz	225 ml
10 fl oz	300 ml
12 fl oz	350 ml
14 fl oz	400 ml
15 fl oz	450 ml
16 fl oz	475 ml
18 fl oz	530 ml
1pt (20 fl oz)	570 ml
1¼ pt (25 fl oz)	700 ml
1½ pt (30 fl oz)	900 ml
1¾ pt (35 fl oz)	1 ltr

American Cup Conversions

AMERICAN	IMPERIAL	METRIC
1 cup flour	5 oz	150 g
1 cup caster/ granulated sugar	8 oz	225 g
1 cup brown sugar	6 oz	175 g
1 cup butter	8 oz	225 g
1 cup sultanas/raisins	7 oz	200 g
1 cup ground almonds	4 oz	110 g
1 cup uncooked rice	7 oz	200 g
1 cup grated cheese	4 oz	110 g
1 stick butter	4 oz	110 g

Oven Temperature

GAS MARK	°F	°C
1	275°F	140°C
2	300°F	150°C
3	325°F	170°C
4	350°F	180°C
5	375°F	190°C
6	400°F	200°C
7	425°F	220°C
8	450°F	230°C
9	475°F	240°C

If using a fan oven you will need to reduce the oven temperature in a recipe by 20 degrees

Liquid Conversions

IMPERIAL	METRIC	AMERICAN
½ fl oz	15 ml	1 tbsp
1 fl oz	30 ml	1/8 cup
2 fl oz	60 ml	¼ cup
4 fl oz	120 ml	½ cup
8 fl oz	240 ml	1 cup
16 fl oz	480 ml	1 pint

ACKNOWLEDGEMENTS

It truly takes a village to write a cookery book, and there are some villagers whom I would like to single out.

Siobhan O'Donovan and Conor Stevens presided over the project from the outset (you can catch the breadth of their interests on their site Mr & Mrs Stevens). Richard and I met them each month for a year, teasing out ideas and moving towards a coherent concept. It was always a joy to climb the steep stairs to their Temple Bar office, knowing that home baking and inspiration awaited. They share a wit but are joyfully independent on their views on just about everything. They have a wonderful capacity to draw out ideas rather than impose their own, no easy feat. As the project developed, Conor's copywriting skills came to the fore: his capacity to lift a sentence with the change of a single word was often mesmerising (he would probably change this word). Siobhan's design accommodated both my wish to have some continuity from my first book as well as new ideas for this one. Her gentle patience was a marvel. She was tireless in the last weeks getting the book to the point that we were all happy.

After our foray into food photography for my first book, fashion designer and friend Liz Quin and I were even better prepared. We had been like magpies, always on the look out for plates, cutlery and props and this time we were fully ready when it was time for the shoots. All the food was cooked in her kitchen and then set up in her back garden, ready for photographer Joanne Murphy who is now well used to our ways and our packed schedule. Joanne was tireless in her efforts to get the best shot. She has a unique eye for what will work in a food shot and this makes her without question the best food photographer in the country. Liz and I travelled on to London with the photos to work with Mark Robson and his colleagues at Altaimage, another extraordinary day of learning. Particular thanks to Ray Gaubert for burning the midnight oil. It now just remains for us to go back to Rosalia D'Aprano and her team in Verona to get the book printed. They take on our books with such enthusiasm. When Liz and I see the pages come off their gigantic presses, it will be a moment of enormous satisfaction.

I have relied heavily on the team at the cookery school during this endeavour. Thanks to Richard Gleeson and Eric Oppenheim for early support and to Fiona Stevens for helping to keep the school running in my absence. Sally Herron was not directly involved in this book but she is the soul of the school and her commitment and integrity are the foundation for a project such as this. Tara Livingston and Noureia

reliable. I would like to thank them both for their tireless dedication and the care they took in preparing all the dishes for the photo shoots. In less able hands, these tasks could have been stressful but they matched their attention to detail with good humour and wise suggestions.

I had some fascinating talks with Caoileann Murphy, postdoctoral research dietician at University College Dublin. In an area of so much misinformation, it is such a breath of fresh air to talk to someone who has such a sound knowledge of this area. Thanks also to Ellen Butler and Judy Leyden for some interesting suggestions.

I am grateful to the many chefs on whose ideas I constantly draw. A particular thanks to John Wyer, Rossa Crowe, Barry Fitzgerald and Sunil Ghai – friends and sources of inspiration.

My husband Richard needed a hook to get interested in the book. When he started to see it as a resource for our three children as they make their way in the world, he threw himself in to the project with tireless energy. Only I will know how much he contributed and how much this is a result of our combined efforts. He has always been a fearless cook. Maybe, with the help of this book, his food can become a little less terrifying.

ABOUT THE AUTHOR

Lynda Booth is a hugely experienced chef who has worked around the world in an array of kitchens, from simple bistros to Michelin star restaurants. She has relished the contrast of working beside Raymond Blanc at Le Manoir in Oxford one year and cooking her way down the Italian Riviera the next. As owner/operator of the renowned Dublin Cookery School, she leverages her vast network of contacts to host her food heroes from home and abroad. A prominent figure at Taste of Dublin, she also makes regular guest appearances on TV and radio. Her first book *"From Lynda's Table"* was a finalist in the World Gourmand Cookbook Awards.

ABOUT DUBLIN COOKERY SCHOOL

Dublin Cookery School has won the Irish Cookery School of the Year (Irish Restaurant Awards) twice over the last four years. It has been praised as offering "cutting edge classes in a gorgeous cutting edge space" (Bridgestone Guide). The school hosts weekend and evening classes and prides itself on the three month full-time certificate course which attracts students from all over the world. It is currently celebrating its tenth year.

To find out more about Dublin Cookery School: www.dublincookeryschool.ie.

Fearless Food by Lynda Booth
Published in 2017 by DCS Publishing

DCS Publishing, 2 Brookfield Terrace, Blackrock
Co. Dublin, Ireland

Text © Lynda Booth 2017
Additional text by Richard Booth
Food Photography © Joanne Murphy 2017
Photos page 6 and 302 © Gary Belcher 2017
Photo page 303 © Simon Burch 2013

A CIP catalogue record for this book is available
from the British Library.

Food styling by Liz Quin and Lynda Booth
Designed in Ireland by Mr and Mrs Stevens

Printed and bound in Italy by Graphicom S.r.l
Colour origination by Altaimage, London

ISBN 978-0-9926951-1-8